The Seventies

An illustrated
History in colour
1970-79

By John Edwards

Macdonald Educational

The Seventies

Contents

First published 1980
Reprinted 1983
© Macdonald Educational Ltd
Macdonald & Co (Publishers) Ltd
Maxwell House, Worship Street
London EC2A 2EN

ISBN 0 356 06788 2 (cased)
ISBN 0 356 06789 0 (limp)

Printed in Great Britain by
Purnell & Sons (Book Production) Ltd
Paulton, nr. Bristol
A member of the BPCC plc

The seventies was a decade of surprises. The economic balance of world power changed dramatically as a result of the oil crisis. From 1973 onwards, the price of oil went up and up. Inflation brought fears that the world was heading for the worst slump since the depression of the thirties.

Young people could no longer look forward to a future of prosperity and full employment. Youthful protest swung away from politics and towards a new concern for the environment.

Advances in technology such as automation, nuclear power and supersonic flight were all regarded as mixed blessings. Even in space, the spectacular advances of the sixties gave way to steadier and more patient exploration in the seventies.

There were surprises in international affairs too. Two deadly enemies, China and the United States, developed a growing friendship. Israel and Egypt signed a peace agreement to end 30 years of mutual hostility. Meanwhile, in South-East Asia, communist Vietnam invaded her communist neighbour, Cambodia.

There were new crazes in leisure activities. Skateboarding and hang-gliding brought thrills and spills, while the punk revolution brought startling innovations to the worlds of fashion and pop music.

But behind everything loomed the energy crisis, affecting rich and poor nations alike. The sixties had been thought of as swinging years. The seventies were more sober.

▲ **Take-off!** A young enthusiast demonstrates his skill at the new art of skateboarding which swept the West in the seventies.

▶ **Take-off!** Concorde came into service in the seventies as the world's first supersonic passenger plane.

The Superpowers

Fear of a nuclear war dominated the international diplomacy of the United States, China and Russia.

▲ **Leonid Brezhnev,** the leading Soviet statesman. Relations between Russia and China worsened during the seventies, but Russia pursued a policy of *détente* (easing of tensions) with the West.

▼ **President Nixon shakes hands with Chairman Mao** during his historic visit to China in 1972. For years their nations had been deadly enemies. But China needed allies against Russia and turned to the West for support.

American and Russian leaders held long negotiations to ease tensions between their nations. In 1972, they arrived at an agreement to limit the arms race. It was known as the Strategic Arms Limitation Treaty (SALT 1).

After six more years of bargaining, a second agreement (SALT 2) was signed. This aimed to limit both sides to a total of 2,250 long range bombers and missile launching systems, allowing each side to suffer a surprise attack and still be able to retaliate.

But the US Senate did not ratify SALT 2 immediately. Critics argued that it favoured the Russians. It gave them superiority in Europe, since it only covered long range nuclear weapons, not those aimed at European cities.

Furthermore, it did not ban the development of new weapons or the modernization of old ones. Above all,

it was hard to ensure that the treaty would be observed.

The communist Warsaw Pact nations had a three-to-one superiority over the Western NATO countries. However, a new weapon was developed in the United States: the neutron bomb. This was a small H-bomb which killed people without destroying buildings; radiation from it cleared up in seconds.

In the built-up European theatre of war its advantages were obvious. President Carter delayed deploying the neutron bomb as a gesture of good faith in trying to limit the arms race.

However, all these careful negotiations were dramatically upset late in December 1979. Russian troops suddenly invaded neutral Afghanistan to quell a threatened Muslim takeover. Fear of a new wave of Soviet expansion placed the arms agreements in jeopardy. The seventies ended in an atmosphere of acute tension.

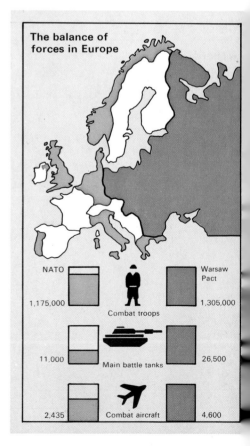

The balance of forces in Europe

NATO		Warsaw Pact
1,175,000	Combat troops	1,305,000
11,000	Main battle tanks	26,500
2,435	Combat aircraft	4,600

▲ **Soviet armoured vehicles on display** in 1977 during celebrations to mark the 60th anniversary of the Russian Revolution.

THE MILITARY BALANCE

◀ **Map** showing the military superiority of the communist Warsaw Pack countries over the forces of Western Europe's NATO (North Atlantic Treaty Organization). The figures are for 1977–8.

▶ **Diagram** showing the nuclear balance between the United States and the Soviet Union under the SALT 1 agreement, in 1976.

There are various ways in which nuclear warheads can be delivered. They can be dropped by bombers or launched by missile from land, sea or air. Certain systems even allow a single missile to carry up to ten different warheads, each directed at a different target.

SALT 2 proposes that at the end of 1981, the two superpowers should restrict their overall number of delivery systems to 2,250.

ICBM: Intercontinental Ballistic Missile (a missile with a range of more than 6000 km).
SLBM: Submarine Launched Ballistic Missile.
MIRV: Multiple Independently Targetable Re-entry Vehicle (a vehicle which allows missiles to carry more than one nuclear warhead, each of which can be aimed at a different target).

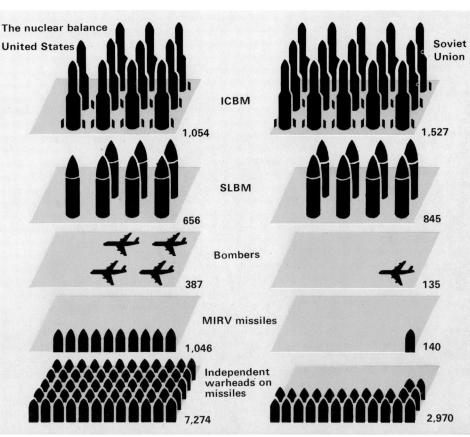

The nuclear balance
United States

Soviet Union

	United States	Soviet Union
ICBM	1,054	1,527
SLBM	656	845
Bombers	387	135
MIRV missiles	1,046	140
Independent warheads on missiles	7,274	2,970

The Watergate Crisis

In November 1972, Richard Nixon was re-elected President of the United States by the largest majority that an American president had ever enjoyed. The future looked bright for his administration.

▲ **Jubilant Republicans** celebrate Nixon's nomination in 1972. He beat the Democratic candidate, George McGovern, by a huge majority. Nixon's foreign policy was popular. He was healing the rift with China and negotiating peace in Vietnam.

But during the election campaign, five men had been arrested for breaking into the Watergate building in Washington. This was the campaign headquarters of the Democratic Party, Nixon's political opponents.

The burglars were arrested and the matter seemed closed. But two young reporters on the *Washington Post* followed up the story. They revealed that the burglars had been trying to plant listening devices in the building. Men at the highest level of Nixon's administration had known of the break-in and had ordered "hush money" to be paid to the burglars for their silence.

Meanwhile, Vice-president Spiro Agnew was forced to resign in October 1973 because of a quite separate scandal involving illegal payments. For the next year, hardly a week went by without some new and damaging revelations about the administration.

The Watergate case went to the courts. Was the president himself involved? Nixon had recorded all his conversations at the White House from an early date. The tapes might clear the matter up, so the courts demanded to hear them.

Nixon stalled. When the courts finally managed to prise the tapes from his grasp, they confirmed his involvement in the cover-up.

Faced with impeachment (accusation of treason) by Congress, Nixon finally resigned in August 1974. Vice-president Gerald Ford took his place.

Watergate had left its mark. The Republicans were discredited, and Ford was defeated by Jimmy Carter, a religious-minded southern Democrat, in the presidential elections of 1976.

Throughout the United States there was a feeling of drift and a lack of confidence in the nation's leaders. The Vietnam War had split America in the sixties. Watergate disillusioned it in the seventies.

▲ **The Watergate building,** campaign headquarters of the Democratic Party. It turned out that the break-in was financed by an organization called CREEP (Campaign to Re-elect the President). This was directed by members high up in Nixon's White House staff.

◀ **Keep Punchin' Mr President!** A billboard poster put up by a Baltimore bar owner called Al Flora. Until the last days of the Watergate crisis, many people refused to believe that the president could have been involved.

▼ **The weariness of defeat** is clearly seen in this picture of Nixon, taken during a face to face interview with Britain's David Frost after the president had resigned.
"I screwed up terribly," Nixon declared. "I let the American people down."

"It's no use looking at me, Spiro. Convincing alibis don't grow on trees, you know."

▲ **Cartoon of 1973.** While the Watergate crisis began to boil, Vice-president Spiro Agnew resigned over an income tax scandal. These and other affairs gave the impression that corruption was rife in the highest offices in the land.

Agnew was replaced by Gerald Ford, a decent but little known Republican who succeeded Nixon after the president resigned.

The Middle East

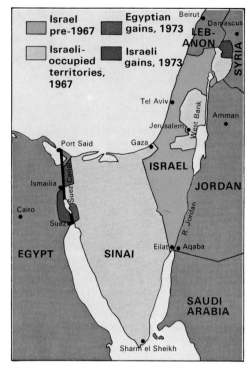

The ceasefire position, 1973. Israel had gained some territory from Syria and Egypt, but Egypt had regained territories in Sinai on the east bank of the Suez Canal. The position was stalemate. Israel had not increased her massive gains of 1967.

Wars between Arabs and Israelis had ravaged the Middle East since 1947. The Israelis had won in 1948, 1956 and 1967. In 1973, war broke out yet again.

On 6 June 1973, Egyptian troops suddenly swept across the Suez Canal. The attack took the Israelis by surprise because they were celebrating the Jewish holiday of Yom Kippur.

But after early Egyptian victories, the Israelis hit back hard. They crossed the Suez Canal themselves and, in the north, they pushed back Syrian forces nearly to Damascus.

Henry Kissinger, the US Secretary of State, managed to negotiate a cease-fire and eventually paved the way for a truce between Israel and Egypt.

No-one had really won the war. Egypt's President Sadat had gained respect among the Arab states for his near success. But the Palestinians (Arab refugees from Israeli-occupied territories) were still bitterly discontented. They launched new raids on Israeli settlements and new terrorist acts to draw attention to their cause.

Terror, and Israeli reprisals, continued. Then in 1977, Sadat announced that he was willing to have peace talks with Israel. Israel's new prime minister, Menachem Begin, took up the challenge. Both countries were weary of a war which meant a third of their budgets being drained by military spending.

The two men held a series of summit meetings, receiving crucial help from the US president, Jimmy Carter. A *Framework for Peace* was finally signed in 1978, and Israel began to withdraw her troops from Sinai (which she had occupied since the Six Day War of 1967).

Israel now enjoyed a new understanding with Egypt, but not with the other Arab states. Most of them fiercely denounced Sadat for betraying the Palestinians. Peace in the Middle East has still not been achieved.

THE PALESTINIAN PROBLEM

◀ **Palestinian guerillas** in the mountains of southern Lebanon.

The Palestinians were refugees who had fled to neighbouring Arab states when the state of Israel was established in 1947.

There were over a million of them, living in ramshackle camps. Many hoped to return to their homeland one day, and their armed guerilla units posed permanent problems to both Israel and their Arab hosts.

In 1974, Palestinians in the Lebanon grew impatient with peace talks following the Middle East War. Armed clashes broke out with the forces of the Lebanese government.

The unrest led to a full scale civil war between the Arab half of the population and Christians who feared an Arab takeover.

Israel claimed that the fighting had led to a build-up of Palestinian guerillas on her own borders. She invaded southern Lebanon and only withdrew when a United Nations peacekeeping force was sent to the area.

▲ **An Israeli tank** in action in 1973. Israel was heavily outnumbered in tanks, troops and aircraft by the Arab forces equipped by the Soviet Union. For example, she had only 1700 tanks to Egypt's 2600 and Syria's 2000.

Israel suffered heavy losses in the first three days of war. Nevertheless, she was able to launch an effective counter-attack.

▼ **The Camp David talks, 1978.** Israel's prime minister, Menachem Begin, America's President Carter and Egypt's President Sadat meet in the United States to talk peace.

Henry Kissinger had already eased tensions by travelling between Israel and Egypt in two years of patient "shuttle diplomacy". Carter continued in his tradition.

The *Framework for Peace* provided for Israeli withdrawals from Sinai, and a United Nations peacekeeping force to be maintained in the area. Sadat was denounced by other Arab leaders. Begin faced fierce criticism from some Israelis who considered Sinai essential to their defence. Israelis had already built settlements to colonize the area.

Oil and Iran

When the seventies opened, scientists were already warning the industrialized nations that they were using up the world's oil resources much too fast.

Since World War Two, oil for industry and transport had been fairly cheap to obtain. As a result, the economies of the industrialized nations had been able to grow steadily.

But after the Middle East War of 1973, the Arab oil-producing nations doubled the price of oil. They also threatened to withhold oil supplies from countries aiding Israel. For the first time, oil's true importance was recognized and it became a weapon in international politics.

Meanwhile, the organization of oil-exporting countries (known as OPEC) agreed to limit the production of oil so that they would not use up their reserves too quickly.

Oil prices soared for the rest of the decade. An energy crisis had arrived, bringing lower industrial production and higher inflation and unemployment throughout the world (see pages 60-61).

Some countries already had their own oil supplies. Others were finding new sources: Norway, Mexico and Britain for example.

But despite the new finds, the world still needed more oil than was being produced. In 1979, it was short of 2.3 million barrels a day.

The United States was the most lavish user of oil, taking up a third of the world's 60 million barrels a day. *Save Energy* campaigns were launched in many countries and governments sped up their search for alternative energy sources.

▲ **A familiar sight in the seventies.** Reduced oil supplies and the disruptions of the Middle East War brought repeated petrol shortages during the decade.

▼ **Ships pump water at an oil rig in the North Sea.** The first oil from Britain's fields was piped ashore in 1975 and reduced her dependence on foreign supplies.

▲ **Iranian students** demonstrate in support of the Ayatollah Khomeini. The strength of religious feeling in Iran (and in neighbouring Afghanistan) took the superpowers completely by surprise.

▼ **Rioters overturn a bus.** Iran's revolution alarmed neighbouring Arab kingdoms. In 1979, Muslim fanatics stormed the holy mosque in Mecca, increasing instability in the area.

▼ **An officer embraces the Shah** as he leaves Iran. The Shah went into exile in Mexico, but then moved to the United States to receive medical treatment for cancer. The Ayatollah's supporters wanted him brought back to Iran and tried for the torture and repression of his opponents, but he died in Cairo in 1981.

Revolution in Iran

Iran was one of the world's biggest oil producers, and the United States relied heavily on her supplies.

But throughout 1978, opposition to the 37-year-old rule of the Shah was mounting. He had wanted to make his country a westernized industrial state but the pace of change was too fast. Muslim and communist leaders united in demanding his overthrow during months of rioting and unrest.

The inspiration behind the revolution was a religious leader, the Ayatollah Khomeini, who lived in exile in Paris. In March 1979, Iran voted to become an Islamic republic. The Shah fled and the Ayatollah returned to hail the new republic as the "first Government of God".

Khomeini's supporters denounced the corruption of the old regime and attacked western customs and dress. Students besieged the American embassy in Tehran, holding its staff hostage. They demanded that the Shah be returned from exile in America, to face trial. President Carter refused, and stopped American imports of Iranian oil.

By December 1979, the deadlock had still not been resolved. Fears of a worsening energy crisis arose with increasing instability in the Arab nations of the oil-rich Persian Gulf.

The Environment

Advanced technology can cause pollution on a frightening scale. The seventies brought a growing spirit of concern for the environment.

▲ **A massive oil spill from the supertanker *Amoco Cadiz*.** The ship was wrecked off the west coast of France in 1978. Thousands of tons of crude oil seeped from the tanker, and the "black tide" affected nearly 200 kilometres of the Brittany coastline.

In 1972, a group of international industrialists produced a computer forecast on how the world environment would be affected by future economic growth. Their report was called *Limits to Growth* and it convinced many people that there was a crisis.

A series of disasters highlighted the dangers to the environment. The village of Seveso in Italy was poisoned by dioxin gas which had escaped from a chemical factory. There were oil spills from tanker collisions and leaking oil rigs. Faults were discovered at nuclear power stations.

Environmental groups sprang up, campaigning to keep the air, rivers and oceans clean. They fought to protect wildlife, to save historic buildings from the bulldozer and the countryside from the motorway.

Some environmentalists took up subsistence farming, shunning modern aids like chemical fertilizers. The general public became much more concerned about what they ate. New consumer groups emerged, and Health Food stores appeared in high streets.

The threat to world resources led many environmental groups to recommend recycling of paper and glass to save valuable raw materials. Both manufacturers and consumers were urged to collect their empty bottles instead of throwing them away.

In Europe, a "Green" party was formed, demanding new legislation to meet environmental needs. In the United States much radical protest against the Vietnam War switched to concern for the environment. In particular, a strong movement against the use of nuclear power sprang up.

Care for the environment was not shared everywhere. The poorer countries of the Third World tended to regard all economic growth as a blessing, whatever the cost to the environment. But in general, a new spirit of concern had taken root.

▲ **Scientists in protective clothing** gather plastic bags holding the bodies of animals killed by a poison gas cloud. It escaped from a chemical plant at Seveso in Italy. The whole village had to be evacuated.

▶ **The sperm whale** was one of many species threatened with extinction as a result of over-intensive hunting.

▼ **This cartoon** suggests that the real endangered species is humanity itself. Careless treatment of the environment could bring disaster.

"Must we? They're already in danger of becoming extinct."

THE WHALE
BOYCOTT WHALE PRODUCTS
WRITE TO YOUR MP: BAN WHALE OIL IMPORTS
SUPPORT YOUR LOCAL FRIENDS OF THE EARTH

SAVE IT

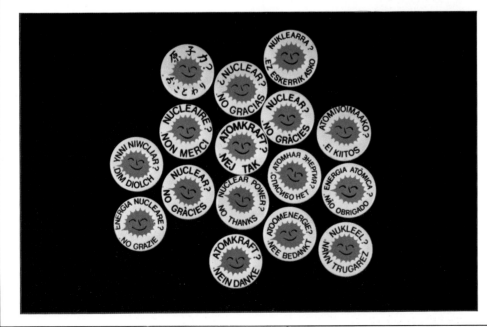

THE NUCLEAR DEBATE

◀ **Nuclear Power? No Thanks.** These badges are in 16 different languages, but the message is the same.

One problem was disposing of long-lived, highly radioactive nuclear waste. Another major problem was plutonium. This fuel was used in certain reactors known as "fast-breeders". Since it was also used in making nuclear bombs, there was always the fear that terrorist groups might obtain supplies of it.

The nuclear programme in the United States suffered a setback after an accident at the Three Mile Island plant near Harrisburg, Pennsylvania. Radioactive steam and gas escaped for several days, leading to the evacuation of all people living within an eight kilometre radius.

No one died of radiation at the time, but campaigners insisted that no more nuclear plants should be built.

Fashion

The seventies were bewildering years for fashion. There was no single trend. Clothing styles had become largely a matter of individual taste.

As always, there were passing crazes. Hotpants were all the rage for women at the beginning of the decade. These skimpy shorts were often worn with ankle-length maxi coats to emphasize the dramatically high hemline (and to provide warmth in colder climates).

Films had a particular influence on what people wore. Woody Allen's comedy *Annie Hall*, for example, brought in a vogue for loose-fitting jackets and baggy "peg-top" trousers for women.

A series of nostalgic films brought back the styles of earlier decades. *The Boyfriend* re-introduced the twenties look, while *Grease* brought back the fifties. By 1979, there was even a mod revival, associated with the film *Quadrophenia* (the mods were the neat, short-haired, scooter-riding dandies of the early sixties).

Pop music had an enormous impact. David Bowie and other superstars of the middle years of the decade wore startling face make-up and glittering outfits which were emulated by their fans in the streets.

When punk rock arrived in 1976, there was a widespread vogue among dedicated enthusiasts for bizarre hair-styles, torn clothes, and accessories such as belts and chains which were designed to startle and outrage. The most dramatic innovation was the safety-pin—worn through the nose.

One fashion did not change. Jeans were the international uniform of the young, with denim jackets, waistcoats and skirts as extras. Western jeans were so prized by youngsters in Eastern Europe that, in 1979, American jean-makers were negotiating with the Soviet Union to set up factories there.

▲ **Hotpants, 1971.** After the mini skirts of the sixties, they were one way of taking the hemline higher still without becoming indecent. Later, hemlines tended to drop and skirts could be worn at almost any length.

▶ **Punks** began by deliberately mocking fashion. Crude colours and synthetic materials were often combined with zips, chains and black leather. But these effects soon became fashions in their own right.

◀ **Traditional Finnish knitwear** adapted to modern clothes. Folk patterns and natural materials became popular as alternatives to synthetic and mass produced clothing.

▶ *"The trousers are about the thirties, the bow tie is about the forties, the jacket is into the fifties, and that's what the seventies is all about."*

This cartoon pokes fun at the nostalgic revivals. Films about earlier decades (and old films re-run on television) influenced these vogues. But perhaps they also reflected a general uncertainty about the present and future.

▼ **Fashion** influenced by Woody Allen's *Annie Hall*. This loose and comfortable style was well suited to the liberated women of the seventies.

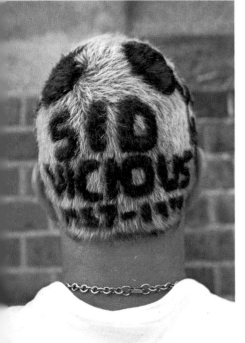

▲ **This punk hairstyle** pays tribute to pop star Sid Vicious who died in 1979. Some punks stiffened their hair with shoe polish or dyed it in violently contrasting colours.

Transport

Developments in transport were deeply affected by the needs to save fuel and protect the environment.

▲ **This cartoon** presents Concorde as an environmental hazard. Because of opposition from environmental groups, it was a year before the Americans would allow the plane to land in New York. Some countries banned flights altogether. Pressure from environmentalists was having effect.

▼ **Tickets and brochures for Concorde.** Flights were expensive and tickets cost more than an ordinary first-class fare on a normal airliner. Although Concorde was a superb engineering achievement, manufacturing and running costs were too high to make it profitable.

The Anglo-French Concorde came into service in 1976. It was the world's first supersonic airliner and could fly passengers faster than a rifle bullet travels —without spilling their drinks.

But because of the noise it caused as it broke the sound barrier, Concorde aroused much opposition from environmental groups. Its routes were restricted, since some countries would not let it fly over their territory.

Concorde was costly to make and terribly expensive to run in the age of high fuel prices. Too few planes were sold to make it a commercial proposition, and no more Concordes were built after 1979.

Passengers really wanted cheaper, rather than faster, air travel. A British businessman called Freddie Laker gave it to them with his cut-price Skytrain service to the United States. A trip to New York became cheaper than one to a European capital.

On the railways, new High Speed Trains made inter-city travel much quicker. On the roads, bicycles made a big comeback. They were handy in traffic, needed no fuel, and were popular with keep-fit enthusiasts.

The energy crisis had enormous impact on motoring. The United States government passed laws to encourage making cars that used less petrol. There was a boom in the sale of small cars, and Japanese models did particularly well.

Shapes changed too. The wedge design was the most efficient because it reduced fuel consumption by lessening wind resistance.

The energy crisis led to renewed interest in electric cars run by batteries. Their drawbacks were their low speed and the short life of their batteries. (More powerful batteries would be much too heavy to be practicable.)

All the same, some manufacturers believed that electric cars would be used widely in the eighties for short-distance travel in big cities.

◄ **Wedge-shaped Swiss Pilcar** of the late seventies. It was one of the most efficient electric cars produced, but the weight and short life of its batteries made it unsuitable for long-distance travel.

▼ **Honda Civic,** one example of the small-engined Japanese cars which became enormously popular in the seventies. Japanese cars sold so well in Britain that the government had to ask Japanese manufacturers to limit their exports.

▼ **Bike it!** Environmentalists recommended cycling as a clean, energy-saving form of transport. Collapsible bikes were produced for easy carrying.

▲ **Freddie Laker,** a British businessman who set up his own airline. The price of air fares used to be fixed by international agreement. Laker fought a successful legal battle with the British and American governments to slash fares across the Atlantic. The success of his Skytrain started a price war among airlines.

The New China

In the sixties, China had developed under the rigid control of Mao Tse-tung, isolated from the rest of the world. But in the seventies, she began to look outwards.

▲ **Wall posters in Shanghai.** They were a traditional way for private citizens to air their views in public. The turmoil after Mao's death caused a wave of poster campaigns, some attacking the government itself.

In 1979, new regulations declared "it is forbidden to disclose state secrets, fabricate information and make false charges, to commit libel and conduct other activities that violate the law."

Even before Mao's death, China had begun to seek foreign allies in her continuing conflict with Russia. She also needed to buy western know-how in order to modernize.

When President Nixon arrived in China in 1972, his visit ended 20 years of hostility to the United States.

Both Mao and Chou En-lai, China's two legendary leaders, died in 1976. A struggle for power followed in China. The left wing was headed by Mao's widow, Chiang Ch'ing, while the right was represented by the army.

The right wing won. They sped up development of China in a programme known as the Four Modernizations. Agriculture, industry, science and technology were marked out for improvement, and foreign aid was sought.

Chiang Ch'ing and three associates (known together as the Gang of Four) were arrested in 1976.

Now China really began to look outwards. In 1978, she resumed diplomatic relations with the United States. Trade agreements with Europe and Japan followed. China opened her doors to tourists and welcomed cultural exchanges with orchestras and theatres from the West. Sporting contacts increased; foreign soccer teams visited China.

The Chinese were hungry for foreign books. English editions of Shakespeare went on sale and sold out in hours. Western clothes began to be seen. Once again, girls could wear dresses instead of the standard Mao tunics.

Mao's doctrines were quietly played down by the new leaders, Hua Kuofeng and Teng Hsiao-p'ing. In Peking, some wall posters appeared attacking Mao himself, though the new leaders clamped down on dissidents who openly attacked the government.

Complex changes were taking place. But one thing was clear. China was determined to develop from a backward giant to a modern superpower.

▲ **Taking snapshots** became increasingly popular among the Chinese as more consumer commodities were made available.

▼ **Eating ice-cream** was a new luxury permitted as the government allowed western influence to enter everyday life.

▲ **Poster attacking the Gang of Four.** Mistakes made during the last years of Mao's rule were blamed on them.

Mao's widow, Chiang Ch'ing, was the leader of the group. She was criticized for her high-handed ways, her personal abuses of power and for damaging production by preventing China's development as a modern power.

▼ **China's new leaders** survey a model for a new agricultural complex as part of the Four Modernizations programme.

Vice-chairman Teng Hsiao-p'ing is second from the right in this group. He visited the United States and even attended a rodeo where he was photographed wearing a cowboy hat—events which would have been unthinkable under Mao.

India and Pakistan

Two powerful personalities dominated the troubled affairs of the Indian sub-continent: Mrs Gandhi of India and President Bhutto of Pakistan.

▲ **Map** showing West Pakistan (now Pakistan) and East Pakistan (now Bangladesh). This oddly divided nation had been created when India was given independence in 1947, because both regions had large Muslim populations while India was mainly Hindu. But the division caused administrative problems from the beginning.

▼ **Young Bangladeshi guerillas** in training during the struggle for independence.

In 1970, the Muslim state of Pakistan consisted of two separate regions, the East and the West. India lay between them.

East Pakistan had close ties with India and resented being dominated by the Western region. At Pakistan's general election of 1970, the East voted solidly for an independence movement headed by Sheikh Mujibur Rahman.

The West's vote was solidly for Zulfikar Ali Bhutto who wanted to keep Pakistan united.

After nine months of violent unrest between the two regions, India came to the aid of the East and waged a two-week war against West Pakistan. India's victory was swift. East Pakistan was made independent and renamed Bangladesh.

For Pakistan, the war had been a disaster. But Bhutto formed a government and in the next six years he did much to restore national pride. He negotiated the release of 90,000 prisoners of war held in India and started a series of economic and political reforms. It was the longest ever period of civilian rule in Pakistan.

But Bhutto had made many enemies. In 1977, he was accused of rigging the general election. In the turmoil that followed, the army took over in Pakistan for the third time since independence in 1947.

The new leader, General Zia ul-Haq, charged Bhutto with plotting to assassinate a political opponent. In 1979, after long deliberation, the courts had Bhutto put to death.

The execution brought protests from many world leaders. But Zia's military government showed no signs of giving up power. Pakistan ended the seventies with political unrest and economic problems still dogging the country.

▲ **Starvation in Bangladesh, 1970.** The region faced appalling problems at the beginning of the decade. Before war broke out, the worst cyclone of all time hit the area. It caused floods which destroyed the rice crop.

About a million people lost their lives, and a similar number later fled as refugees to India. Relief organizations such as the Red Cross and Oxfam could barely cope.

▲ **A communist rally in India** during the unrest of 1975. The Russian-backed Communist Party supported Mrs Gandhi.

Mrs Gandhi in India

In 1975, Mrs Gandhi had been Prime Minister of India for nine years. But scandal surrounded her government. The courts barred her from holding office for six years because of election frauds.

Mrs Gandhi declared a State of Emergency, claiming she needed special powers to deal with unrest in the universities and strikes in industry. For 21 months she ruled almost as a dictator before announcing a general election.

It was bitterly fought. Mrs Gandhi's forced sterilization programme to deal with overpopulation brought fierce opposition. It was said that some men were rounded up at random and sterilized against their will. The influence of her son, Sanjay, also aroused hostility.

The opposition united against her Congress Party and won decisively. It was a triumph for democracy, because many had thought that India's 300 million voters would be too afraid to vote against the government.

But after 1977, the newly formed coalition began to fall apart, unable to cope with inflation, unemployment and strikes. Mrs Gandhi began to make a political comeback. (In fact, she was re-elected prime minister by a massive majority in 1980.)

India's politics remained unstable. But despite all her problems, the country was still the world's largest parliamentary democracy.

▲ **Zulfikar Ali Bhutto** was the son of a wealthy Pakistani landowner and had been educated at Oxford. In 1971 he became the first civilian president of Pakistan.

▶ **Indira Gandhi** was the daughter of India's first prime minister, Jawaharlal Nehru. Critics accused her of pursuing family interests by promoting her son, Sanjay.

Vietnam and Cambodia

For 20 years, North Vietnamese guerillas had waged war on the government of South Vietnam. The South relied heavily on American support in order to survive.

▲ **American troops** in Vietnam cheer on hearing that the United States intends to withdraw from the country. The war had become bitterly unpopular. The last troops left in 1973, though America continued to supply arms to South Vietnam.

▼ **Panic, 1975.** An American official punches a man in the face as he tries to board a plane already overloaded with refugees from the South. As the communists arrived, thousands of South Vietnamese fled the country, about 130,000 going to the United States.

In 1969, however, President Nixon announced that the United States would withdraw all her troops from South Vietnam. Four years later, the last American troops left the country.

The military balance swung in favour of the North Vietnamese. Supported by Russia, they invaded the South. Half the rural population of the South fled to the cities, her armies collapsed and the country was overrun. In 1976, North and South were united under a single communist government.

The new Vietnam faced a huge task of post-war recovery, and a harsh regime was set up. The South was required to provide food and raw materials for the North. Its swollen cities were emptied, and people were forced back to work on the land in labour camps.

Food shortages were common. About 200,000 political opponents of the new regime were imprisoned.

The government also began to expel the Chinese community from Vietnam. This led to increasing tensions with China itself.

Though China had supported the communist struggle, Vietnam had been a traditional rival for over 2000 years. Russian influence in Vietnam added to Chinese fears, and the tensions erupted in a short border war between China and Vietnam in 1979.

The result of these upheavals was that hundreds of thousands of refugees fled Vietnam: Chinese, middle classes, intellectuals, even peasants and fishermen.

Many left in small boats, heading for Malaysia and Hong Kong, and many died at sea in their ramshackle craft. The sheer number of the surviving "boat people" was so great that neighbouring countries could not cope. They had to appeal to the United Nations to try and solve the problem by distributing the refugees among countries all around the world.

CAMBODIA

▶ **A Khmer guerilla celebrates victory.**
Communist guerillas, known as the Khmer
Rouge, took over Cambodia in 1975.

Their fanatical leader, Pol Pot, launched
a campaign to empty the crowded capital
of Phnom Penh and force people back to
the villages. Any opposition was met with
furious violence.

In four years under Pol Pot, 2 million
Cambodians were executed or died from
disease or malnutrition.

Throughout this grim period, Cambodia
was involved in clashes with Vietnam.
China lent support to Cambodia to counter
the growing strength of the Vietnamese.

In 1978, Vietnam invaded Cambodia and
the Pol Pot regime collapsed. The
Vietnamese installed an occupation army
and set up a government favourable to
themselves. Some Khmer guerillas fought
on, but the appalling barbarity of their
regime had lost them their friends abroad.

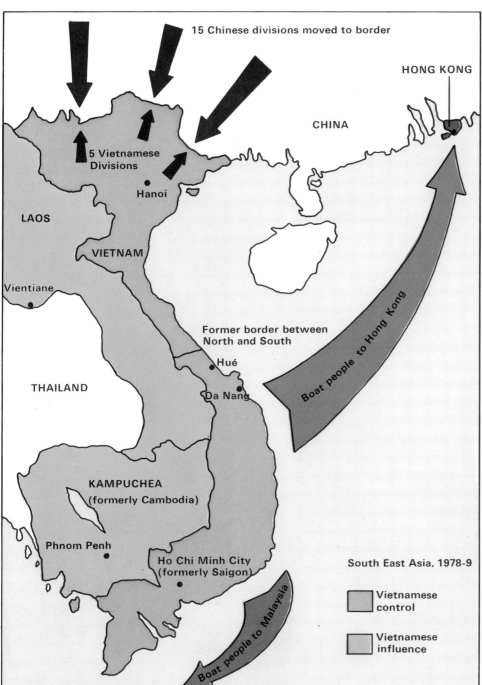

15 Chinese divisions moved to border

HONG KONG

CHINA

5 Vietnamese
Divisions

Hanoi

LAOS

VIETNAM

Vientiane

Former border between
North and South

Hué

Da Nang

THAILAND

Boat people to Hong Kong

KAMPUCHEA
(formerly Cambodia)

Phnom Penh

Ho Chi Minh City
(formerly Saigon)

Boat people to Malaysia

South East Asia, 1978-9

Vietnamese
control

Vietnamese
influence

◀ **In 1975, North Vietnamese forces overran
South Vietnam** and the two regions were
united. At the same time, communists took
effective control of Laos, relying on
Vietnamese support. In 1979, Vietnam overran
Cambodia, further extending its influence.

Western leaders feared for the security of
Thailand and neighbouring countries.

China also feared the Vietnamese upsurge.
Vietnam was a traditional enemy, and
hostilities between the two countries erupted
in a brief border war in 1978–9.

▲ **Plight of the boat people.** It is estimated
that about a quarter of a million refugees may
have drowned, starved to death or been
murdered by Thai pirates.

The exodus was originally stimulated by
the Vietnamese government who wanted to
get rid of what they called "undesirables"—
mostly Chinese or middle-class residents.

But towards the end of 1979, a new wave
of true escapees, on the run from the
Vietnamese authorities, began.

Sport in the Seventies

International sporting events reached larger and larger audiences through global television coverage.

Television created mass audiences for sports such as gymnastics which had only had a limited following before.

A 14-year-old Russian gymnast called Olga Korbut became known world-wide for winning three medals in the 1972 Munich Olympics. It was headline news four years later when an even younger girl, Nadia Comaneci of Rumania, scored maximum points for perfect performances at the Montreal Olympics.

The East Germans were the rising stars of the Olympics, winning 66 medals in 1972, and no less than 90 at Montreal in 1976.

Political prestige counted greatly in international events. There was widespread concern that athletes were using drugs to improve their performances. A Scottish footballer was sent home from the 1978 World Cup in Argentina for using illegal stimulants.

Football was the world's fastest growing sport and even began to sweep the United States. Many international stars such as Pelé of Brazil and Beckenbauer of West Germany were imported to boost attendances. Soccer was organized with all the commercial flair and showmanship associated with America's own national sports.

Commercial sponsorship entered tennis, which had become a professional game in 1968. Tennis stars such as America's Jimmy Connors and Sweden's Bjorn Borg became the highest paid sportsmen of all.

Even cricket, which had always been a stronghold of amateurs, was wrenched into the business world. An Australian tycoon called Kerry Packer shocked cricketing circles by forming his own World Series Cricket organization. Top players were lured from traditional events by massive cash offers, to play on floodlit pitches wearing coloured flannels.

▲ **Nadia Comaneci,** Rumanian gymnastic star of the 1976 Montreal Olympics. Gymnastics won mass audiences because of television coverage.

▼ **Cartoon** illustrating fears that drugs were being widely used in athletics to improve performances.

"I've had that, you fool—where's the baton?"

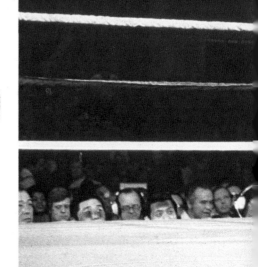

▲ **Pelé of Brazil playing for Cosmos,** a United States team which also included Beckenbauer from West Germany and Chinaglia from Italy. The pitch is made of synthetic Astroturf.

▲ **Bjorn Borg of Sweden** won a record four men's singles titles in a row at Wimbledon from 1976 to 1979. He was known as the ''ice-cool Swede''.

◀ **Muhammad Ali,** the only man to win the world heavyweight boxing title three times. He is seen here defeating Leon Spinks in New Orleans, 1978. Ali was 36 years old.

New Crazes

New crazes swept the western world in the seventies. As so often in the past, most of the popular fads began in the United States.

▲ **A skateboarder** leaps off the ramp at El Cajon National Skatepark, California, wearing helmet, gloves and pads.

Skateboarders developed their own slang. Crashes were only too frequent; they were known as "pavement pizzas".

Keeping fit had become an obsession with many Americans, and one craze dominated all others: jogging (running at a relaxed pace). Streets, parks and open spaces suddenly filled with people jogging singly, in pairs, or on massive "fun runs".

Enthusiasts maintained that there was no better exercise. Critics suggested that the craze put too much strain on the heart. It could cause more ills than it was supposed to forestall.

Their claims seemed to be borne out when President Carter collapsed on a highly publicized jog near Washington in 1979. Fortunately, he recovered; and he vowed to keep on jogging.

An entirely new sport, skateboarding, emerged in the seventies. It spread so fast and became so sophisticated that its supporters wanted it to be included in the Olympic Games.

Protective clothing for skateboarders filled sports shop windows, and skateboard parks were built for young enthusiasts. But as the eighties approached there were signs that the boom was over. Roller skating came back, and combined with disco-dancing to create the new art of "roller disco".

Hang-gliding was another new sport, and one which satisfied man's age-old ambition to fly. A motorized hang-glider even flew the English Channel.

But crashes, even from modest heights, caused several deaths and serious injuries. The dangers of hang-gliding led to pressure for an official body to enforce safety controls. "Windsurfing" on surfboards equipped with sails offered excitement with fewer obvious risks.

On some beaches, topless bathing became acceptable. Topless models also appeared in popular newspapers, and nudity in general had become less shocking. But it could still startle when practised by "streakers". They would dash stark naked through public places to astonish the onlookers.

▲ **Yoga,** another aspect of the health craze, offered mental as well as physical well-being.

▲ **Hang-gliders** could stay in the air for hours by riding the thermals (warm air currents).

▶ **Roller disco** combined discotheque dancing with roller skating to create a new craze.

▲ **President Carter,** in shorts and track suit top, jogs in the grounds of the White House.

▶ **Windsurfing** needed considerable strength as well as skill.

Films and Television

In the sixties, it had seemed that television would kill the film industry. But just when Hollywood seemed to be in its death throes, the cinema made a comeback.

▲ **World-famous stars of the Muppet Show:** Kermit the Frog, Miss Piggy, Fozzie Bear, the Great Gonzo and others.

These animated puppets were created by a British company, but given American accents to win television audiences in the United States. The characters were sharply observed and appealed to adults just as much as children.

Hollywood turned to producing cheap films for television. It also began to make spectacular films that made cinema-going a real event. Subjects were often too shocking, and their treatment too expensive for television companies to handle. Cinema attendances increased for the first time in 20 years.

The Exorcist started a vogue for terrifying supernatural stories. Disaster movies like *Jaws* were huge box office successes. And *Star Wars*, a science fiction epic, became the most successful film of all time.

Film stars still drew the fans: Paul Newman, Clint Eastwood, Barbra Streisand and Faye Dunaway, for example. But in the big blockbusters, sensational subject matter was often more important than the stars.

Current events were quickly adapted for the screen. Several films were made about the Entebbe Raid (see page 55), and the Watergate Affair was filmed as *All the President's Men. The China Syndrome* described a nuclear disaster and appeared in the same year as a radiation leak occurred at the Three Mile Island nuclear plant.

Sex was presented more openly than ever before, and there was a new tendency to glamorize violence, in films as different as Stanley Kubrick's *Clockwork Orange* and the Kung Fu films of Bruce Lee.

West Germany came to new prominence in film-making with its young directors, Fassbinder, Wenders and Herzog. A new wave of film makers also emerged in Australia, with Peter Weir's *Picnic at Hanging Rock*.

But television was still the most popular entertainment medium. A ring of stationary satellites now made it possible to beam live pictures to and from anywhere in the world.

American television series had worldwide audiences, and some had deep impact: *Roots* and *Holocaust* for example. On a lighter note, the stars of Britain's *Muppet Show* became internationally famous.

Television became more adaptable. TV games could be played, and video cassette recorders now allowed viewers to record shows and replay them time and time again.

SATELLITE COMMUNICATION

▶ **Television signals** only travel in straight lines. But the earth is round and the signals will not pass through it. To send pictures from one part of the world to another, a satellite is needed. It receives signals from one place and transmits them to another.

The first communications satellite was called Telstar and was used to transmit pictures across the Atlantic in 1962. In 1970, Telstar provided live world-wide coverage of the World Cup in Mexico. About 800 million people saw Brazil beat Italy in the final.

Today, improved satellite systems are in constant use, not only for major events but to provide live news pictures giving instant global coverage of current events.

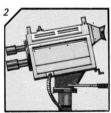
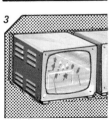

▲ **Instant communications.** Four cameras at a stadium (**1** and **2**) feed pictures to a mixing studio. A producer watches them on monitors (**3**).

He switches from camera to camera to get the best shots. These are fed along a landline to a satellite station (**4**) beaming them into space.

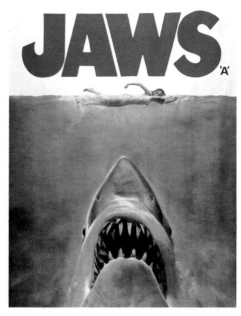

JAWS 'A'

▲ **Poster for** *Jaws,* a film about a killer shark, 1975.

▲ **Charles Bronson** starred in this film version of the Entebbe Raid, made shortly after the event.

▶ *Star Wars* broke all box-office records.

▼ *The China Syndrome* featured Jane Fonda, a leading opponent of nuclear power.

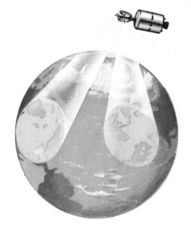

▲ **The satellite** reflects the television signals to another part of the earth. (The satellite shown here is Intelsat IV which began operating in 1974).

The signals are received at a special ground station (**5**) and are again monitored in a studio (**6**). The result is fed to the main transmitting aerials (**7**).

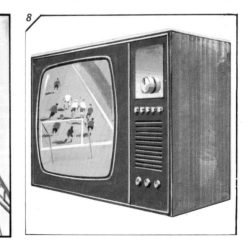

Finally, the signals are converted into pictures by the cathode ray tube inside a television (**8**). The whole operation takes barely a second.

Pop Music

Pop music had immense international appeal. Even communist countries admitted western bands.

▲ **Swedish pop group Abba.** They won the Eurovision Song Contest in 1972 and went on to achieve immense international success

▼ **Paul McCartney, his wife Linda and Denny Laine** pose with a few of their gold discs. McCartney survived the break-up of the Beatles and gained a new generation of fans with his group, Wings. His overall royalties made him the best-selling songwriter of all time.

Elton John visited Russia and the Bee Gees were invited to China. New stars like Rod Stewart and David Bowie became million sellers, while established performers like Bob Dylan and the Rolling Stones retained their appeal. So did Elvis Presley, whose death in 1978 was mourned by millions.

Rock had become big business, and live groups used massively expensive equipment on stage. Experimentation with electronic effects also made rock more sophisticated. But by 1976, a reaction had set in.

New Wave bands set out to recover the simplicity and raw energy of earlier years. These "punk rockers" wrote earthy, deliberately shocking lyrics. Britain's Sex Pistols even recorded with Great Train Robber, Ronald Biggs.

Black West Indian reggae became popular. The music was associated with Rastafarianism, a Jamaican religion based on the worship of Emperor Haile Selassie of Ethiopia.

Another trend was the craze for disco music whose insistent rhythms were said to approximate the beat of the human heart. The craze began with

the film, *Saturday Night Fever*. Its star, John Travolta, also featured in *Grease*, a film which revived nostalgia for the music of the fifties.

No group had quite the impact that the Beatles had had in the sixties. But one Beatles member, Paul McCartney, achieved massive success with his new group, Wings. By 1979, he had become the best-selling songwriter of all time.

▲ **Bob Marley,** wearing the distinctive ''dreadlock'' hairstyle of the Rastafarians. (Notice the portrait of Haile Selassie, projected in the background.) The lyrics of Rastafarian reggae emphasized black oppression by a white society which they nicknamed Babylon.

◀ **John Travolta in** *Saturday Night Fever*. He was a particular favourite with younger fans.

▶ **Sid Vicious,** a member of the punk rock group, the Sex Pistols. In 1978 he was arrested on suspicion of murder, and died of a drug overdose while awaiting trial.

▼ **A variety of LPs by New Wave bands:** Sham 69, the Buzzcocks, the Jam, Blondie, the Clash, Ian Dury and Elvis Costello. They restored a raw feeling of reality to pop music at a time when it seemed to be being swallowed up by glamour and big business.

Western Europe

In 1972, Denmark, Ireland and Britain joined the European Economic Community (EEC or Common Market).

▲ **Britain's Conservative prime minister, Edward Heath, signs the Treaty of Accession** to the Common Market in Brussels, 1972.

The Treaty came into force officially on 1 January 1973. Denmark and Ireland joined at the same time but Norway stayed out.

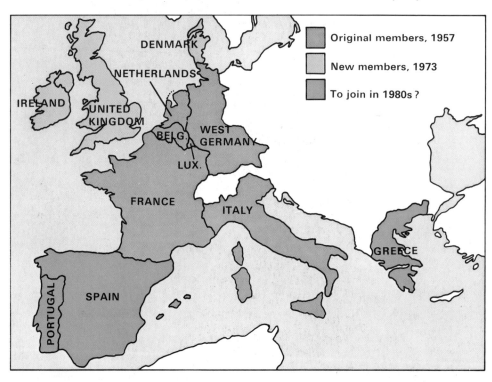

Original members, 1957

New members, 1973

To join in 1980s?

DENMARK

NETHERLANDS

IRELAND

UNITED KINGDOM

BELG.

WEST GERMANY

LUX.

FRANCE

ITALY

GREECE

PORTUGAL

SPAIN

▲ **The Common Market of the 1980s** is likely to include Spain, Portugal and Greece. There are also many Norwegians, Swiss and Austrians who would like their nations to join.

Opponents of the Market complain that membership involves a loss of sovereignty (control of one's own affairs). Supporters believe this is balanced by greater unity.

Membership of the Common Market was fiercely debated in Britain. In 1975, Harold Wilson's Labour government put the issue of whether to stay in to the people in Britain's first ever referendum; the answer was a clear Yes. (In contrast the Norwegians voted in 1972 to stay out.)

There were strong differences among the nine member states. Seventy per cent of the EEC budget, raised by taxes, went on agriculture. Much of it went to help the small farmers of France and Germany. Both Britain and Italy complained that this was unfair to them.

The agricultural policy produced odd effects. Too much butter was produced, and the huge surplus was nicknamed the Butter Mountain. It could not be sold cheaply *inside* the Common Market, because EEC policy guaranteed high prices to farmers. So it was sold to Russia for much less than EEC members paid themselves.

Yet the benefits of membership still appealed. Portugal, Spain and Greece all moved from dictatorship to democracy in the seventies, and all three were expected to join the Common Market in the early eighties.

Portugal's dictatorship was overthrown in a left-wing army coup in 1974. Although succeeding governments were unstable, predictions of a communist takeover were not fulfilled.

Spain's dictator, Franco, died in 1975 and the country moved peacefully to a parliamentary democracy under a restored monarchy.

In Greece, the seven-year rule of the colonels fell in 1974, and parliamentary democracy was restored. However, relations with Greece's old enemy, Turkey, were as bad as ever. The Turks invaded Cyprus in 1974, and occupied the northern region. There were disputes over territorial rights in the Aegean Sea, where oil was discovered.

◄ **Catalan nationalists** demonstrate in Barcelona, Spain. While Western Europe seemed to be moving towards greater unity, regional groups *within* individual nations pressed for more local control.

In Spain, Basque and Catalan nationalists were active. In Britain, Scotland and Wales both demanded greater self government.

▼ **A boy celebrates the Queen's Silver Jubilee** during a street party in Britain, 1977. The 25th anniversary of Elizabeth II's coronation brought a massive outpouring of popular enthusiasm for the monarchy.

But Britain faced problems. Her industry was in decline, unemployment was high and inflation was soaring.

▲ **A black youth** arrested during anti-racist demonstrations in Britain. There were some outbreaks of racial tension, but no great support for the right-wing National Front.

▼ **Victim of the terrorist Red Brigade,** shot dead during the kidnapping of former Italian prime minister, Aldo Moro. Italian politics were disturbed by terrorist violence.

Eastern Europe

The Soviet Union still dominated her allies in Eastern Europe. Increasing prosperity was accompanied by demands that basic human rights should be respected.

▼ **A director of the Polish Coca-Cola factory** displays a sales award while scanning the party newspaper. Eastern Europe developed new trade links with the West, but consumer goods were still in short supply.

East Germany remained the most loyal of Russia's allies, but Rumania began to go her own way. She would not put her army under Russian control, nor increase her defence spending on Russian orders. More and more she looked to China for support.

There were still shortages of food and consumer goods in Eastern Europe. In Poland, massive price rises in 1971 and 1976 led to widespread demonstrations by workers, peasants, students and Church leaders. Moves were made to encourage private enterprise in shops and farms.

Czechoslovakia remained a strong focus for dissident activity (dissidents were people who opposed rigid Soviet control of political and cultural life). Russia had invaded the country in 1968 to restore pro-Soviet government. In 1977, a group of dissidents set up a movement called Charter 77. They declared that they would look out for and report all violations of human rights.

Charter 77 received a lot of publicity in the West, and forged links with other dissidents in Eastern Europe. The Czech government replied by imprisoning many Charter 77 leaders, including the playwright, Vaclav Havel. Supporters were often fired from their jobs and found it hard to get any kind of work.

In Russia, the battle for human rights had never been fiercer. The leading rebel was the author, Alexander Solzhenitsyn. Although he went into exile in 1974, other dissidents took up his work. One was the scientist, Andrei Sakharov. He was awarded the Nobel Peace Prize in 1975, but was not allowed to collect it.

The Soviet authorities imposed harsh prison sentences on dissidents. Despite new contacts with the West, internal repression continued.

▶ **Polish film poster.** It advertises an Italian film, *The Conformist*, about life in Fascist Italy. But it also says much about life under any regime where the press is censored and free speech is rigidly controlled.

Latin America

Most of Latin America was governed by military dictators. Civilian governments and revolutionary movements fell to the generals.

In Chile in 1970, a Marxist called Salvador Allende became the first democratically elected communist head of state in the world.

He began to nationalize banking and Chile's main industries: copper, coal and iron. He also took land away from the big landowners and distributed it among the peasants.

But these measures took place amid soaring inflation and social disorder. There were threats of a right-wing coup, and workers' militias were formed to defend Allende's government.

In 1973, rioting broke out in Chile's main cities. The army seized power and besieged Allende and his supporters in the presidential palace. Allende died during the fighting.

The new military government of General Pinochet became notorious for the torture and persecution of political opponents. About 2000 of them simply "disappeared", while hundreds of others remained, untried, in prison. The general promised no further elections until 1985.

In Brazil, the army had ruled continuously since 1964, and remained in power throughout the seventies. It showed no sign of handing power back to civilians, though some limited political activity was allowed.

In Argentina, Juan Peron made an amazing comeback. He had ruled as a dictatorial president from 1946 to 1955, when he was overthrown by the army. In 1973, he returned from exile in Spain to become president again.

His second wife, Isabel, was made vice-president, but she was never loved by the people as his legendary first wife Eva ("Evita") had been.

When Peron died in 1974, Isabel succeeded him. In two years, Argentina fell into anarchy and economic ruin. Five people a day died in the street violence between left and right wing terrorists. Inflation rose to 500%. In the end, the army seized power again.

▲ **A Sandinista guerilla in Nicaragua.** For 50 years, the country had been ruled by the dictatorship of the Somoza family, supported by the United States. Somoza controlled the 20 largest companies, owned a quarter of the arable land, and had a personal fortune of 500 million dollars. But in 1977, guerillas overthrew the dictatorship in a civil war. It was the only successful Latin American revolution of the decade.

▲ **The Panama Canal** had been controlled by the United States since 1903 when building began. She also controlled the Canal Zone, two strips eight kilometres wide on each side. Panama had resented this for years. In 1978, President Carter returned the canal to Panama. The United States no longer wished to police the area as openly as before.

▶ **Map of Latin America.** The army had ruled the largest country, Brazil, since 1964. In Chile and Argentina, civilian government fell to the generals during the seventies.

Uruguay had always been famous for its democratic institutions. But the activities of left-wing Tupamaros guerillas led to the gradual introduction of army rule.

▼ **Troops with captured Allende supporters** taken during fighting in the streets of Chile, 1973. Altogether, more than 7000 prisoners were rounded up and held in the capital's sports stadium—including 200 foreign correspondents and cameramen. The mistreatment of untried political prisoners brought storms of international protest.

▲ **Juan Peron with his wife Isabel,** a former cabaret dancer ignorant of politics. When she came to power, Argentina fell apart while she took guidance from an astrologer. Peron's first wife, Eva, had been a much more important political force, and a musical about her life was a smash hit in the seventies.

Medicine

The successes and failures of scientific medicine came sharply into focus. New technology was available, but a more questioning attitude to drugs emerged.

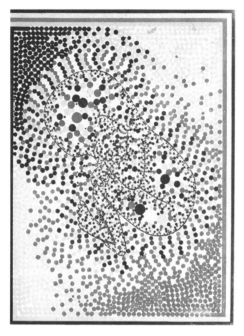

▲ **Scan picture of an unborn baby** inside its mother's womb. The body scanner greatly improved pre-natal care for expectant mothers. It was also used widely for the detection of brain tumours and cancer.

▼ **Helping a patient to give up smoking** Governments discouraged smoking. Even the Chinese, the world's heaviest smokers, started an anti-smoking campaign. But the problem facing all governments was that taxes on tobacco were an important source of income and not easily replaced.

On 25 July 1978, a girl called Louise Brown became the world's first "test-tube baby". An egg from her mother's body had been successfully fertilized in a laboratory. For childless couples the technique brought new hope.

Was it possible to manipulate human reproduction even more dramatically? Scientists developed "cloning" in the seventies. This is a means of reproducing several identical living things from a single original. Gardeners have practised it for centuries by taking cuttings from one plant to produce others.

Scientists did manage to clone frogs, and people suggested that it might be possible to clone humans too. Ira Levin examined the idea in his novel *The Boys from Brazil*. In it, cells from Hitler's body are implanted in women around the world to create a whole race of Hitlers.

Despite such grim fantasies, most scientists rejected the idea that a complex organism such as the human body could ever be cloned.

In 1979 Dr Geoffrey Hounsfield won the Nobel Prize for physiology by developing the body scanner. This revolutionized X-ray techniques by scanning the body from all angles in three-dimensional sections.

Drugs came under careful scrutiny. The morning sickness drug, Thalidomide, was found to produce deformed children, and the drug company was forced to pay millions of pounds in compensation.

Doubts also grew about the contraceptive pill. Women over 35 who were heavy smokers were advised not to use it because of dangerous side effects.

In contrast, natural medicine became hugely popular, especially acupuncture (an ancient Chinese method of anaesthetizing patients by sticking pins into points in the nervous system).

The harmful effects of cigarette-smoking were proved. Some governments banned advertisements on television and made manufacturers include health warnings on packets. California held a vote on whether smoking should be banned from all public places. The move was defeated, but it showed the strength of anti-smoking feeling.

▲ **Mother Theresa,** a Catholic nun, won the 1979 Nobel Peace Prize for her work among the sick, the poor and the starving in the slums of Calcutta. Despite advances in technology, the medical problems of Third World countries remained acute.

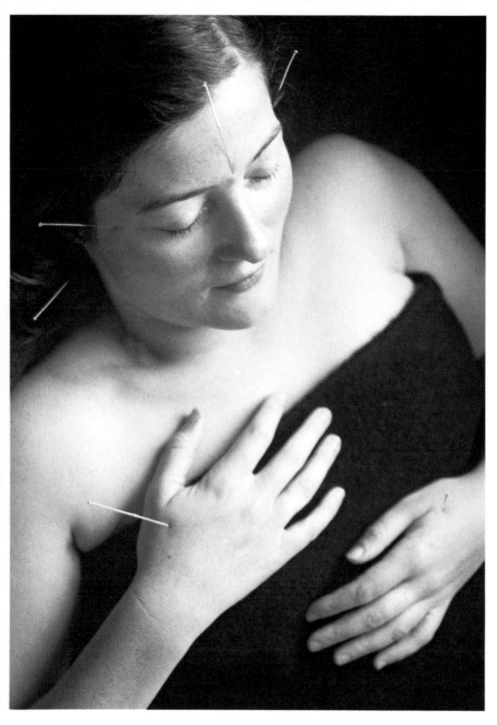

▲ **A Dutch victim of Thalidomide.** The drug, prescribed to ease nausea, was found to produce deformed babies.

◀ **The ancient art of acupuncture.** The technique became popular in the West after China began to open its doors to foreigners in the early seventies.

THE FIRST TEST TUBE BABY

▶ **Louise Brown, the first test tube baby,** was born in Oldham, Lancashire. Her parents, Lesley and John Brown, had tried for nine years to have a child, but could not because of a blockage in Lesley Brown's fallopian tubes. This meant that the female egg cell could not be fertilized by the male sperm to cause pregnancy.

Two British doctors, Patrick Steptoe and Robert Edwards, perfected a way of removing a ripe egg from the woman, placing it in a laboratory dish and adding the husband's sperm. After incubation of the fertilized egg, they put it back into the mother's uterus.

It was not a foolproof technique. Difficulties at every stage had led to many failures. But Louise Brown crowned ten years of experiment for the two doctors.

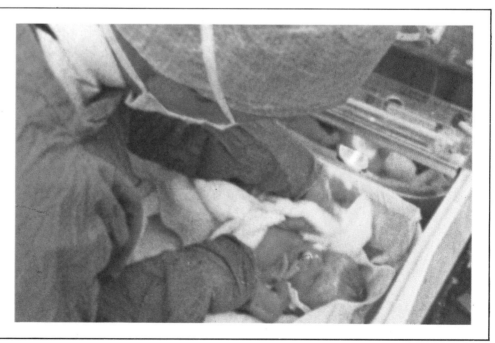

Religion

Two traditional religions, Roman Catholicism and Islam, caught the public eye in the seventies. New cults also sprang up, and some of them had sinister features which aroused public concern.

The Islamic faith was boosted by the new wealth of the Arab oil-producing nations. There was a resurgence of faith in Iran, Pakistan, Afghanistan and in several African states.

In these areas, westernization had often disrupted communities, and now people returned to the traditional values of Islam with enthusiasm.

In Iran, the Ayatollah Khomeini tried to order society according to the Koran (the holy book of Islam). Pakistan's General Zia introduced laws deriving from the Shari'a (the Islamic code of justice). Traditional punishments such as public flogging were meted out to criminals.

The Catholic Church also came to public attention. The Latin Mass was abolished, and radicals even wanted to permit contraception, abortion and marriage for priests.

For Catholics, 1978 was a year of surprises. Pope Paul VI died and was replaced by Pope John Paul I. But after only one month, the new pope died too. His replacement was Karol Wojtyla, a Polish cardinal, who took the name John Paul II. He was the first non-Italian pope for 455 years, and he came from a communist country.

John Paul II brought a new dynamism to the Church, visiting Poland, Mexico, Ireland and the United States and drawing massive crowds.

Outside the traditional faiths, several new cults sprang up. Some aroused public concern, for their followers were kept in strict communities isolated from the outside world.

One was the Californian church of Jim Jones, which set up a People's Temple commune in Guyana.

In 1978, a delegation of American journalists and politicians investigating the commune were attacked by Jones's followers. Four were killed. Faced with exposure, Jones ordered his followers to commit suicide with him. In a horrific ritual, 913 members died.

41

The Arts

The arts mirrored the mood of the period. Artists still experimented with new forms, but there was a greater seriousness and a desire to reach a broader public.

▲ **Erica Jong,** an American novelist, was one of several new women writers who emerged in the seventies. Her book *Fear of Flying* explored the social and psychological pressures which hindered women from living their lives independently and without guilt.

▲ **Günter Grass,** a German writer. He defended the virtues of humanism against extremists of both left and right. His book *From the Diary of a Snail* (1972) described the 1969 German elections in which he campaigned for the Social Democratic Party.

One writer stood out among the novelists of the period: the Russian dissident, Alexander Solzhenitsyn. His powerful trilogy, *The Gulag Archipelago*, recorded the Russian labour camp system under Stalin.

Solzhenitsyn's continuing criticism of Soviet life led to expulsion from Russia in 1974. He settled in the United States, but was no easier on his hosts than on his home country. In a speech at Harvard University, he accused the West of materialism and "spiritual exhaustion".

Democratic freedoms were also championed by the German writer, Günter Grass, and the English dramatist, Tom Stoppard. Both defended tolerance against extremism.

Nobel prizes went to the American, Saul Bellow, and the Australian, Patrick White. In popular literature, few books had more impact than Frederick Forsyth's *Day of the Jackal* (1971), one of several fictional thrillers set against well-researched, factual backgrounds.

In painting, wild experimentation gradually gave way to greater realism. This was seen especially in the works of David Hockney who delighted in clean lines and good draughtsmanship. In sculpture, however, one abstract work caused a sensation. London's Tate Gallery paid thousands of pounds for a sculpture consisting solely of a flat pile of bricks.

The architectural sensation of the decade was the strikingly modern Pompidou Centre in Paris, a transparent leisure centre described by its critics as looking like an oil refinery.

In music, there were attempts to bridge the gap between classical and popular styles. The classical guitarist, John Williams, teamed up with jazz musicians. The composer, Andrew Lloyd Webber, combined classical with rock in his *Paganini Variations*, and in his hit musical *Evita*, based on the life of Eva Peron.

▶ **Alexander Solzhenitsyn,** Russian novelist and dissident. Despite a distinguished military career in World War Two, he had spent eight years in a labour camp and another four in exile in Siberia.

After settling in the United States in 1974, his strict Orthodox Christianity and outspoken political views disturbed many who had admired his literary genius and undoubted personal courage.

▼ **David Hockney,** an English artist, poses in front of a set he designed for Mozart's opera *The Magic Flute*.

Hockney had experimented with abstract art in the sixties but later produced scenes with sharp contours and a crisp realism.

▲ **The Pompidou Centre in Paris.** Critics described it as a "plastic palace", but 20,000 people a day visited the transparent building which houses museums, exhibitions and a library. One feature of the building was that lifts and stairs were set *outside*.

▼ **The notorious pile of bricks** bought by London's Tate Gallery. The work was by the American sculptor, Carl André, and was called *Equivalent VIII*. It consisted simply of a rectangular arrangement of yellowy brown firebricks placed on the gallery floor.

Science and Technology

Computers were developed in the fifties and lasers in the sixties. But both were dramatically improved to revolutionize technology in the seventies.

Early computer circuits had been controlled by bulky valves. Then scientists invented transistors which shrank their size. In the seventies, the circuits were miniaturized further when they were embedded in tiny chips of silicon.

As computers got smaller and more efficient, they began to take over jobs which had once been performed by people. Factories computerized many of their mechanical processes. Computers entered offices as word processors (machines that could set type faster than any human).

Experimental computers were built for simple medical diagnosis. Patients could feed information about their illnesses to the machines and the machines decided what was likely to be wrong with them.

Computerized teaching machines, telephone switchboards and super-market check-outs were built.

Lasers also became much more versatile. Laser is short for Light Amplification by the Stimulated Emission of Radiation. It is a way of storing light and releasing it all at once to provide concentrated energy.

Lasers were used for industrial drilling, in studying weather and in surgery. The Apollo astronauts beamed lasers at the moon to measure distance and speed.

Lasers created the new art of holography. This is a form of three-dimensional photography created by splitting and reflecting light beams onto film. Scientists suggested that three-dimensional television might come in the eighties.

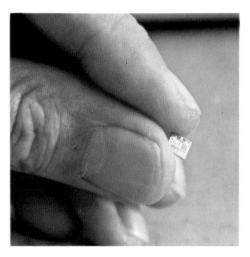

▲ **The mighty micro,** a silicon chip smaller than a postage stamp. In the fifties, a computer as complex as the human brain would have needed to be the size of Greater London. By the eighties, such a machine would be the size of a portable typewriter.

Scientists predicted that micro chips would produce a Computer Revolution as profound as the Industrial Revolution itself.

▼ **Computerized industry.** The Italian car firm, Fiat, launched a car "untouched by human hand". Their Strada model was built entirely by robots.

Computerization was already beginning to threaten jobs in the seventies and to pose serious problems of unemployment for the future.

▼ **A simple solar cooker.** It cooks for nothing, cleanly and quickly—if the sun is shining.

▲ **A laser drill at work in industry.**
   Scientists believed that lasers would transform nuclear power, and that they could be used to start thermo-nuclear fusion (the same reaction that takes place when a hydrogen bomb explodes). The present method involves using powerful electrical discharges.

Alternative energy

Scientists predicted that the world's gas and oil reserves would be almost exhausted within 20 years. The need to save energy and develop new sources became acute.

Nuclear power was one solution, but it provoked fierce criticism (see pages 12-13). While the nuclear debate raged, scientists searched for less dangerous ways of harnessing energy sources.

One method was to build devices which would amplify and store the rays of the sun. Immense installations were built in France and the United States. President Carter even installed solar heating in the White House. But the system was so expensive that it would take 30 years before its cost was paid off.

Wind and sea power were also investigated. In North Carolina, the world's largest windmill provided energy for 500 homes. In Britain and Japan, scientists studied schemes to use the tides to generate electricity. Two small installations were already being used in France and Russia. The search for alternative energy continued.

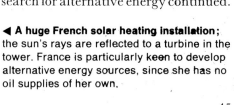

◀ **A huge French solar heating installation;** the sun's rays are reflected to a turbine in the tower. France is particularly keen to develop alternative energy sources, since she has no oil supplies of her own.

Exploring Space

After the moon landing of 1969, exploration continued. But the space race was less competitive and less hectic.

▲ **The surface of Mars,** photographed by automatic cameras on Viking II, 1976. The information sent back by America's Viking I and II missions led scientists to conclude that there was no life on Mars.

There were no plans to land humans on the planets, but patient exploration by unmanned craft continued.

The United States sent five more manned Apollo missions to the moon. The Russians sent unmanned vehicles which sent back samples and information automatically.

In 1975, the first international link-up took place in space, when an American Apollo docked with a Russian Soyuz spacecraft.

It was the last "space spectacular". The sheer cost of the space race had already forced the United States government to cut back its spending. All the same, much patient research went on. There were missions to Mars, Venus, Saturn, Jupiter and Mercury.

Some later Pioneer probes carried information about earth on metal plaques which may one day be seen by intelligent life elsewhere.

Much research was carried out aboard orbiting space laboratories: the Russian Salyut and the American Skylab. Here, astronauts experienced the effects of prolonged weightlessness. They also studied the earth from space, sending back information about weather, plant life and minerals.

America's Skylab, launched in 1973, began falling to earth five years later. The 84-ton craft did not burn up when it re-entered the atmosphere, as scientists had hoped.

The world waited anxiously to see what region would be hit by the debris. In fact, Skylab plunged to earth in 1979, in a remote part of Australia. No-one was hurt.

SALYUT SPACE STATION

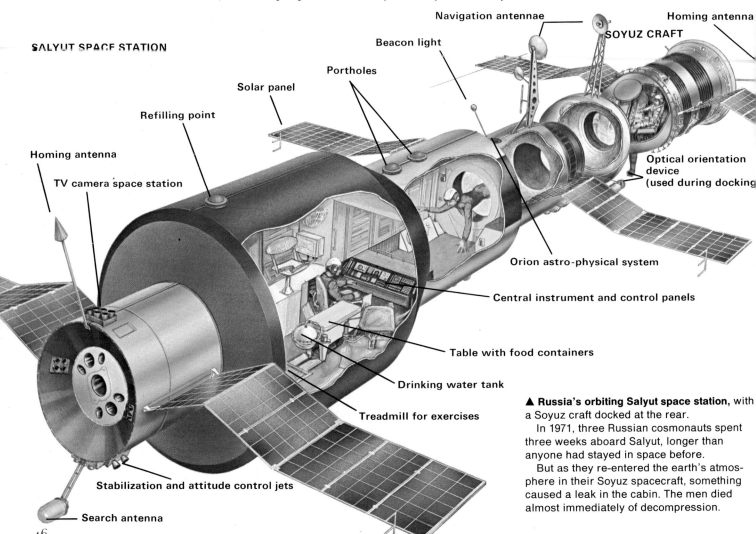

Navigation antennae
Beacon light
Portholes
Solar panel
Homing antenna
SOYUZ CRAFT
Refilling point
Homing antenna
TV camera space station
Optical orientation device (used during docking
Orion astro-physical system
Central instrument and control panels
Table with food containers
Drinking water tank
Treadmill for exercises
Stabilization and attitude control jets
Search antenna

▲ **Russia's orbiting Salyut space station,** with a Soyuz craft docked at the rear.

In 1971, three Russian cosmonauts spent three weeks aboard Salyut, longer than anyone had stayed in space before.

But as they re-entered the earth's atmosphere in their Soyuz spacecraft, something caused a leak in the cabin. The men died almost immediately of decompression.

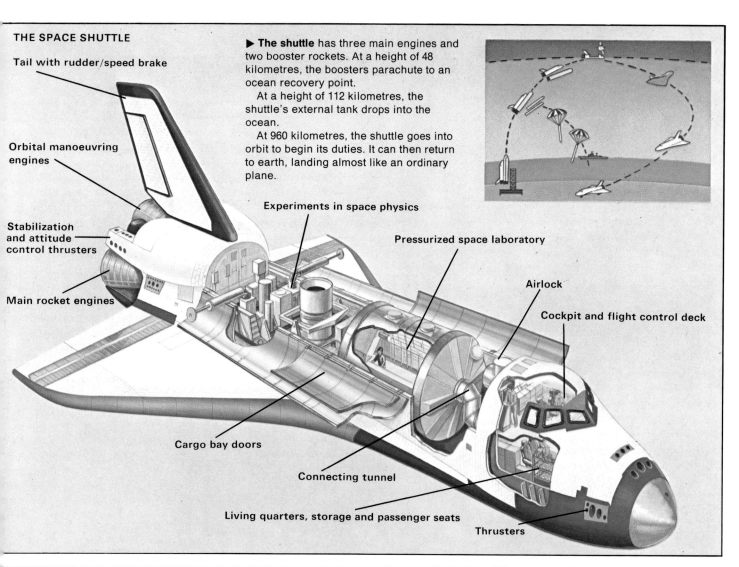

THE SPACE SHUTTLE

Tail with rudder/speed brake

Orbital manoeuvring engines

Stabilization and attitude control thrusters

Main rocket engines

▶ **The shuttle** has three main engines and two booster rockets. At a height of 48 kilometres, the boosters parachute to an ocean recovery point.

At a height of 112 kilometres, the shuttle's external tank drops into the ocean.

At 960 kilometres, the shuttle goes into orbit to begin its duties. It can then return to earth, landing almost like an ordinary plane.

Experiments in space physics

Pressurized space laboratory

Airlock

Cockpit and flight control deck

Cargo bay doors

Connecting tunnel

Living quarters, storage and passenger seats

Thrusters

Stamps issued by the United States and Soviet Union to commemorate the Apollo-Soyuz link-up, 1975. It was the first, and so far the only, international link-up, and was watched by millions of television viewers.

The space shuttle

The Americans aimed to make space travel easier with their space shuttle programme, which was first announced in 1972.

The shuttle consists of two units: the orbiter containing pilots, passengers and cargo; and the booster rockets to lift the orbiter into space.

The orbiter is the size of a modern passenger aircraft. Like an aircraft it has wings. Once in space, it will be able to remain in orbit for up to a month, then return to earth, landing like an aircraft.

The shuttle will be re-usable, and so make space travel cheaper. It will carry a crew of up to seven, undertaking research, helping to build space stations, providing a rescue service for crew in distress, and launching satellites into orbit.

It will also be able to carry out repairs in other craft. (If the shuttle had been ready by 1978, it might have been able to save Skylab before it began to break up.)

The shuttle was first tested in 1977 and it was hoped to launch it in 1979. However, technical problems delayed the project. The first launching was re-scheduled, and took place in April 1981.

Women's Liberation

The women's liberation movement was founded in 1968 and gained widespread support throughout the next decade.

JUICY, FRUITY, FRESH & CHEAP

WELLS Jaffa Orange Drink

▲ **"Sexploitation" in advertising?** Liberated women fiercely objected to images like this. They believed that they presented women simply as glamorous playthings for men. This particular poster caused storms of protest from the women's movement.

Many women had come to feel that society favoured men. Women were seen simply as wives and mothers. Few were expected to have careers, or even ideas, of their own.

Yet the contraceptive pill had given women greater control over child-birth. Mechanization made sheer physical strength unimportant in many jobs. Education had led women to expect more in opportunities than society offered them.

Women's groups sprang up in the 1970s, demanding true equality before the law, in pay, and in employment. Governments were persuaded to introduce laws to help women in these areas. In Britain an Equal Opportunities Commission was set up to monitor progress and receive complaints.

Women began to work in professions which had previously been thought suitable only for men. Women jockeys appeared in horse-racing, and women joined fighting units in the armed forces. In Spain, the first women matadors took part in bullfights.

Women complained that even the use of language needed to be changed. For example, the word "spokesman" implied that the speaker was male. In its place, "spokesperson" appeared.

Being called *Miss* or *Mrs* revealed whether a woman was married or not. Men did not face this problem with *Mr*. The new form, *Ms*, was invented, and became widely used.

Some protests seemed more frivolous. For example, the US Weather Bureau was forced to stop calling hurricanes after women's names alone. Hurricane Elsa made way for Hurricane Bob.

But by the end of the decade, women's liberation had become much more than an oddity or a joke. When Britain's Margaret Thatcher became the first woman prime minister in the Western world, it came as no great surprise. Attitudes to women had begun to change.

◀ **Italian women demonstrate** to "break the chains of oppression". They are dressed casually for their own comfort. Liberationists rejected elaborate clothing and cosmetics which were only designed to appeal to men.

On early demonstrations, brassieres were often burnt as symbols of oppression; uncomfortable and unnecessary to many women. Bra-burning was often mocked, but it was a significant gesture. Women were treating their bodies with a new frankness.

▶ **Germaine Greer,** an Australian-born spokesperson for the women's movement. Her influential book *The Female Eunuch* argued that men had denied women's own sexual feelings while taking all power for themselves.

Other authors included Kate Millett, whose *Sexual Politics* depicted relationships between the sexes as a power struggle; women were sometimes idolized, sometimes patronized, but always exploited.

◀ **A cartoon** pokes fun at the emergence of female matadors in Spain. Liberationists might argue that the cartoon itself exploits women. It implies that they are likely to meet a serious threat with a petty gesture.

Women objected to a number of subtle slights. All might seem unimportant in themselves, but they contributed to an overall pattern in society; women were not taken as seriously as men.

▼ **A woman sergeant** in the Israeli army drills new recruits. As the seventies wore on, women were accepted more and more in roles previously reserved for men.

Mrs Golda Meir of Israel, Mrs Gandhi of India and Mrs Bandaranaike of Sri Lanka had become national leaders in the sixties.

In 1979, Britain's Margaret Thatcher became the West's first woman prime minister. She was closely followed by Dr Maria de Lourdes Pintasilgo in Portugal.

Independent Africa

▲ **Map of southern Africa,** showing the newly independent states of Angola and Mozambique. Marxists took control in both countries. The white governments of Rhodesia and South Africa felt increasingly isolated. Zambia and Mozambique offered shelter to the guerillas of the Rhodesian Patriotic Front who established camps within their borders.

Rhodesia was re-named Zimbabwe-Rhodesia when blacks entered the government. It is now known simply as Zimbabwe.

The last European colonial power withdrew from Africa. Foreign states no longer scrambled for territory, but they did struggle for influence.

When Portugal became a democracy in 1974, her colonies of Angola and Mozambique were granted independence. Communist-backed guerillas took control in both countries.

Fidel Castro's Cuba supplied much aid. Fourteen African nations received a total of 43,000 Cuban troops: a third of all Cuba's forces. East Germans also made their first appearance in Africa as military advisers.

The advance of black government left Rhodesia and South Africa isolated. Both had white rule, and both were important to the superpowers because of their mineral wealth.

Rhodesian whites finally conceded power to a black government in 1979, but held on to many important posts as safeguards.

The Soviet-backed guerillas of the Patriotic Front claimed that the new government was not representative. Though they entered talks in Britain with the Rhodesian government, they also stepped up guerilla raids. Whites left Rhodesia in their thousands.

South Africa looked more secure. It was the wealthiest country in Africa, but pursued a rigid policy of *apartheid* (the separation of white, coloured and black races).

There was growing resentment among the 19 million blacks who outnumbered the whites by four to one. In 1976, serious riots broke out in the black township of Soweto.

Black anger was further inflamed the next year, when the popular young black leader, Steve Biko, died in police hands. At the inquest, the police were cleared of any blame. The verdict was denounced throughout the world as a mockery of justice.

▲ **A white Rhodesian farmer's daughter** is given target practice. The guerilla war went on until late in 1979, when the government and the Patriotic Front agreed to fresh elections which would be supervised by the British. The elections were held in 1980, and Patriotic Front leader, Robert Mugabe, was swept to victory by a massive majority.

◀ **Rioting in Soweto, South Africa, 1976.** The trouble started with an argument over the school curriculum. Students turned it into a children's crusade for black rights. The disturbances spread to Pretoria and over 250 blacks died, many shot by the police.

Apart from racial tensions, South Africa was also hit by a financial scandal known as the Muldergate Affair (after the American Watergate crisis). A minister, Connie Mulder, was forced to resign, and the prime minister Dr Vorster, retired through ill health in 1978.

▼ **Jubilant FNLA soldiers** celebrate Angola's independence in 1975. There were three different nationalist movements in Angola, the FNLA, UNITA and the MPLA.

When Portugal granted independence to Angola, a bitter civil war broke out. Russia and Cuba supported the MPLA with arms and Cuban troops. The United States sent aid to the FNLA via its Central Intelligence Agency (CIA). China supported UNITA.

By 1976, the Marxist MPLA had gained effective control of the country, though FNLA and UNITA guerillas continued to operate in pockets of resistance.

Soviet influence disturbed western leaders, and the United States made renewed efforts to win friends in Africa.

Africa–Two Dictators

Two brutal dictators brought shame to the African continent: Amin in Uganda and Bokassa in the Central African Republic.

▲ **Ugandan Asians.** About 100,000 of them were expelled. Since many were British passport holders, they came to settle in Britain. Their businesses were confiscated, and they had to smuggle out what money they could.

▼ **Public executions in Uganda;** aprons are tied onto two prisoners. Amin often supervised the interrogation and execution of opponents.

Idi Amin seized power in 1971, in a peaceful army coup. At the time, many people hoped he would bring stability to a country weakened by corruption and inefficiency.

It was not to be. The next year, Amin ordered all Asians holding British passports to leave Uganda. Since most of them were businessmen and shopkeepers, the effect on the country's economy was disastrous.

In addition, the main crop, coffee, was neglected. There was a vital lack of food, and inflation soared.

Amin declared himself a Field Marshal and President for Life. Political, tribal and religious opponents were murdered. The whole population was terrorized by Amin's secret police, the State Research Bureau, whose favourite method of killing was hammering their victims to death.

Amin's method of diplomacy was startling. For example, he sentenced an English lecturer, Dennis Hills, to death for referring to him as a "village tyrant". Then he insisted that Britain's prime minister, James Callaghan, flew to Uganda to plead for the man's life.

By 1979, the western powers had broken off relations with his regime. With Uganda falling apart, a joint force of Tanzanian troops and Ugandan exiles invaded the country. Amin fled to Libya, and his troops were defeated after six months' fighting.

Another African dictator, Jean-Bedel Bokassa, was ousted in the same year. He had ruled the Central African Republic with French aid for 13 years. But after an atrocity involving the murder of 100 schoolchildren, France withdrew its support. Bokassa was overthrown and went into exile.

▼ **Idi Amin** wearing the medals he awarded himself. They included the Victoria Cross and all other medals of the British army. He also invented a new order for himself, "Conqueror of the British Empire".

Amin had started his career as a sergeant in the British army, when Uganda was one of Britain's colonies. When he came to power, he took particular delight in humiliating British residents.

Amin was hostile to Israel, so he found some support among Arab leaders, particularly Colonel Gaddafi of Libya. Amin supported the Palestinian cause.

▲ **Jean-Bedel Bokassa** began as a sergeant in the French colonial army, and came to power in a coup in 1966.

Bokassa made himself President for Life and decided to become an emperor like his hero, Napoleon. His coronation ceremony in 1977 cost £10 million and included a Napoleonic throne and a gold crown encrusted with diamonds.

Like Amin, Bokassa delighted in medals, and bestowed on himself titles like First Engineer, and Best Footballer.

He attracted worldwide hostility by taking part in the murder of 100 schoolchildren who were demonstrating against the cost of school uniforms. The uniforms could only be bought from a shop owned by one of Bokassa's wives.

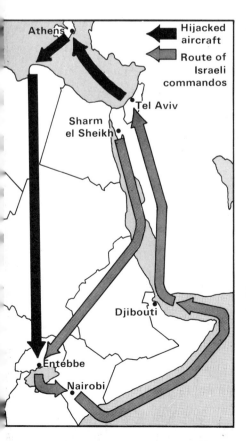

THE ENTEBBE RAID

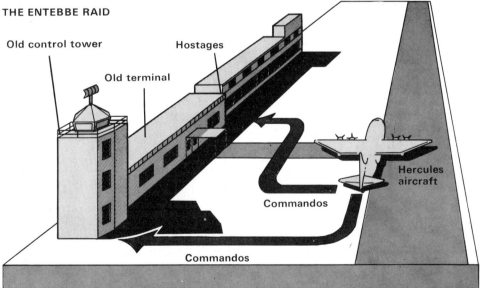

◄ **On 27 June 1976,** a group of West German and Palestinian terrorists hijacked a plane from Tel Aviv as it left Athens. They took the plane to Entebbe, holding the 247 passengers and 12 crew hostage for the release of terrorists held by Israel. The Israelis swiftly prepared an assault force of 200 commandos to rescue the hostages.

▲ **On 3 July,** the assault force flew to Entebbe in three Hercules aircraft. In a brilliant operation, it overpowered the guards, freed the hostages and sped back to Israel. Only two commandos died, while seven terrorists and 20 Ugandans were killed. But one elderly hostage was left, Mrs Dora Bloch. In his fury, Amin ordered her death.

Terror International

▲ **A decade of terror began with a bang** as Arab guerillas blew up three planes at Dawson's Field in Jordan, 1970.

Terrorism became more widespread, and terrorist groups developed international links.

▲ **Soldiers of the IRA (Irish Republican Army)** in training. Their aim was to force British troops to leave Northern Ireland so that the province could be united with the South. In the seventies, their bombings and assassinations spread to England.

The Palestinian movement was the hub of terrorist activity. It had an estimated force of 2,000 guerillas, with bases in Lebanon and Iraq.

The Palestinians also trained terrorists from the West German Baader-Meinhof gang and the Red Army in Japan. Money, arms and information were shared among the groups.

The Baader-Meinhof gang grew out of the radical student movement of the sixties. Members were middle-class rebels with a savage hatred of capitalism, who staged a series of bank robberies to finance their operations.

They cooperated with Palestinians to hi-jack a plane at Mogadishu in Somalia. West German commandos stormed the airliner, killing three of the terrorists and wounding another.

In Italy, the Red Brigade's campaign of terror reached a peak with the kidnapping and murder of the former Italian prime minister, Aldo Moro.

In Ireland, the IRA continued its

campaign to get British troops out by bombings and assassinations. In 1979 IRA terrorists blew up Lord Mountbatten and three others; on the same day 13 British soldiers were killed in another bomb blast.

In Holland, a new group emerged the south Moluccans. They were exiles who wanted independence from Indonesia for the island of South Molucca. In the longest siege of the decade, they held 51 passengers hostage on a train for 20 days, with another 110 hostages in a school nearby. Dutch marines rushed the train, killing six of the nine terrorists. Only two hostages died.

The terrorist threat brought new counter-measures. Special commando groups were trained to deal with hijackings. Psychiatrists were called in to advise on long sieges and kidnappings. In 1977, 17 European nations signed an agreement of cooperation to meet the terrorist crisis. Only time would tell whether they would succeed

The Munich Olympics

Kidnapping for ransom and for the release of imprisoned terrorists became increasingly frequent. Above all, terrorists aimed to strike where they would get maximum coverage in the press to publicize their causes.

In 1972, Palestinian terrorists launched their most publicized attack of all. The whole drama was played out before a world-wide television audience tuned in for the Olympic Games in Munich, West Germany.

Eight Arab terrorists from an organization called Black September forced their way to the Israeli dormitories in the Olympic village.

They shot two athletes dead and took nine hostages, demanding the release of 200 Arab guerillas held by Israel. The terrorists wanted the West German government to fly them by helicopter to a nearby airfield, and then on to a friendly Arab capital.

After tense negotiations, the Germans took the terrorists and their hostages to Furstenfeldbruck airport, 32 kilometres from Munich.

German marksmen were waiting for them. In the gun battle which followed five Arab terrorists were killed and three captured. But the terrorists had killed all nine Israeli hostages.

The event cast a shadow over the Olympics and caused deep embarrassment to the West German government. There was talk of abandoning the Games altogether, but in the end they went on as planned.

▶ **A masked Arab terrorist** at the Olympic village, Munich, 1972.

▲ **Ilich Ramirez Sanchez, better known as "Carlos",** link-man in the international web of terror. He masterminded several daring terrorist coups including the hijacking of Arab oil ministers at a Vienna conference, 1975. He is thought to be living in Libya.

▲ **Patti Hearst,** daughter of an American millionaire, was kidnapped by a group calling itself the Symbionese Liberation Army. She later took part in a bank raid with them. Whether she did so of her own free will, or was brainwashed, has never been clear.

▲ **Hans-Dietrich Schleyer,** wealthy German industrialist. In 1977, he was kidnapped by the Baader-Meinhof gang and offered in exchange for eleven gang members held in prison. When the West German government refused, Schleyer was murdered.

Who Was Who

▲ **Salvador Allende,** Chilean president.

Ali, Muhammad (1942–). Black US boxer. He became world heavyweight champion in 1964 but was stripped of his title for refusing to serve in the US Army because he opposed the Vietnam War. Ali regained the title in 1974, lost it in 1977, but won it for a record third time in 1978.

Allende, Salvador (1908-73). Marxist politician in Chile. He was elected president in 1970, but was opposed by big business and the United States' CIA (Central Intelligence Agency). He was overthrown in an army coup of 1973 and committed suicide in the presidential palace.

Amin, Idi (1926–). Ugandan president. A sergeant under British rule, he became a general after Ugandan independence in 1962. Amin seized power in 1971 while President Obote was abroad. For eight years he terrorized the country until he was overthrown in 1979.

Begin, Menachem (1913–). Right-wing Israeli politician. He had been a terrorist during Israel's struggle for independence in 1946-8. Begin became prime minister in 1977. With Egypt's President Sadat, he was responsible for the Middle East *Framework for Peace*.

Bhutto, Zulfiquar Ali (1928–79). Pakistani political leader. In 1967, he formed the People's Party pledged to Muslim socialism. In 1971 he became the first civilian president of Pakistan, but was accused of ballot-rigging and was overthrown in an army coup of 1977. He was executed in 1979.

Bokassa, Jean-Bedel (1921-). President of the Central African Republic. An army commander at independence in 1960, he seized power in a bloodless coup in 1966. In 1972 he declared himself President for Life, and in 1977, Emperor. He was overthrown with French help in 1979.

Brezhnev, Leonid Ilyich (1906–1982). Russian leader. He became First Secretary of the Soviet Communist Party when Khrushchev was deposed in 1964. He emerged as the strong man in the leadership and became President in 1977.

Callaghan, Leonard James (1912-). British politician. He succeeded Harold Wilson as Labour prime minister in 1976. A moderate, he had some success in restraining inflation in 1976-7, but a wave of strikes against his pay policy led to his defeat in the 1979 election.

Carter, James Earl (1924-). US Democratic politician. Originally a peanut farmer, he became Governor of Georgia in 1971, and defeated Gerald Ford to become president in 1976. He helped bring Israel and Egypt together, but his home policy was criticized for indecisiveness.

Castro, Fidel (1927-). Cuban revolutionary and national leader. Originally a lawyer, he led the successful revolution against Cuba's dictatorship in 1959. He developed strong ties with Russia. In the seventies, he sent over 40,000 Cuban troops to Africa.

Fonda, Jane (1937-). Film star and political activist. She campaigned on behalf of American Indians, Black Panthers, Women's Liberation and withdrawal from Vietnam (broadcasting on Hanoi radio in 1972). She and her husband, Tom Hayden, also became anti-nuclear campaigners.

Ford, Gerald Rudolph (1913-). US Republican politician. He became vice-president on Spiro Agnew's resignation in 1973, and president when Nixon resigned over Watergate (1974). But the Republicans had been discredited, and Ford was defeated by Jimmy Carter in 1976.

Franco, Francisco (1892-1975). Spanish dictator. He defeated the Republicans in the Civil War of 1936-9 and set up a one-party state. For 36 years he did not relax his dictatorship. After his death in 1975, Spain became a constitutional monarchy under King Juan Carlos.

Gaddafi, Muammar (1941-). Libyan leader. He founded the radical officers' movement which deposed King Idris in 1969. He imposed strict Muslim practices on Libya while supporting revolutionary movements abroad, notably the Palestinian guerillas.

Gandhi, Mrs Indira (1917-). Indian politician. She was the daughter of Nehru, India's first prime minister, and became prime minister herself in 1966. Accused of electoral corruption, she declared a State of Emergency in 1975. She was defeated at the polls in 1977, but was returned to power in 1980.

Giap, Vo Nguyen (1912-). Vietnamese Communist general. He had fought both Japanese and French occupiers, achieving a brilliant victory over the French at Dien Bien Phu in 1954. He later led the North Vietnamese to victory against the South. In 1975, he became deputy premier in the new government.

Giscard d'Estaing, Valery (1926-). French president. An aristocrat, he had served as Gaullist Minister of Finance from 1962-74. On the death of President Pompidou in 1974, he succeeded to the presidency, becoming the youngest French head of state for 126 years.

Greer, Germaine (1939-). Australian writer and feminist. In 1971, she wrote one of the most influential books about women's liberation, *The Female Eunuch*. In 1979, she published *The Obstacle Race*, assessing the achievements of female painters throughout history.

Haile Selassie (1892-1975). Emperor of Ethiopia. Crowned in 1930, he was overthrown by Mussolini but returned to Ethiopia in 1941. At the end of his reign, Ethiopia was devastated by drought and famine. He was deposed by left-wing army officers in 1974 and died in 1975.

Heath, Edward (1916-). British Conservative politician. He became prime minister in 1970 and took Britain into the Common Market. The miners' union opposed his incomes policy and went on strike. In the 1974 election which followed, Heath was defeated and resigned.

Hockney, David (1937-). British artist. He was a flamboyant figure of the Swinging Sixties in London, flirting with abstract and Pop art before settling for a more representational style.

▲ **Jimmy Carter** meets Pope John Paul II in the United States.

Hua Kuo-feng (1912-). Chinese Prime Minister. He was little known outside China until he was appointed premier on the death of Chou En-lai in 1976. When Mao died in the same year, he became Chairman of the Central Committee.

John Paul II (1920-). The first non-Italian pope for 455 years. Born Karol Wojtyla in Poland, he fought in the resistance against the Germans in World War II. Later, he became Archbishop of Cracow and a cardinal. He was elected to the papacy in 1978 on the death of John Paul I.

Kaunda, Kenneth (1924-). President of Zambia. He led the movement for independence for Northern Rhodesia which became the new country of Zambia in 1964. He established a one-party state in 1972, and gave shelter to Rhodesian Patriotic Front guerillas.

Khomeini, Ayatollah Ruhollah (1900-). Iranian religious leader. He headed the country's 32 million Shi'ite Muslims, but was expelled in 1964 for opposing the Shah's social and economic reforms. When the Shah was overthrown in 1979, Khomeini returned to set up an Islamic republic.

Kissinger, Henry Alfred (1923-). German-born US diplomat. As Nixon's Special Adviser on National Security (1969-73), his efforts to bring peace in Vietnam won him the Nobel Prize. In 1973, he became Secretary of State.

Mao Tse-tung (1893-1976). Chinese Communist leader. In 1949, he became Chairman of the People's Republic after defeating the Chinese Nationalist army. Mao broke with Russia and set about galvanizing China in the Cultural Revolution of the sixties. In his last years he was treated almost as a god.

Meir, Golda (1898-1978). Israeli politician. She was born in Russia, moved to America, then settled in Palestine in 1921. She served Israel as an ambassador and minister, and became prime minister in 1969. She resigned unexpectedly in 1974, shortly after the Yom Kippur War.

▲ **Henry Kissinger,** US Secretary of State.

▲ **Mrs Thatcher** celebrates election victory.

Moro, Aldo (1916-78). Italian politician. A lawyer by training, he entered politics as a Christian Democrat, was three times foreign minister and twice prime minister. In 1978 he was kidnapped and murdered by terrorists.

Muzorewa, Bishop Abel (1925-). Rhodesian churchman and politician. He became the country's first black prime minister in 1978 after the white government agreed to share power with the blacks. He was bitterly denounced as a "puppet" by Patriotic Front guerillas.

Nixon, Richard Milhouse (1913-). US Republican politician. He was elected president in 1968 and pursued a successful foreign policy of withdrawal from Vietnam, conciliation in the Middle East and friendship with China. Re-elected in 1972, he was forced to resign over Watergate in 1974.

Nyerere, Julius (1922-). Tanzanian leader. He founded the Tanganyika Africa National Union to press for independence, gained in 1961. As president, he supervized the merging of his country with Zanzibar to form Tanzania (1964). He was a leading spokesman for African socialism.

Sadat, Anwar (1912-1981). Egyptian president. In 1952 he took part in the army coup led by Nasser. On Nasser's death in 1970, he became president. He led Egypt in the Middle East war of 1973, but agreed to peace talks with Israel in 1977.

Schmidt, Helmut (1918-). West German Social Democratic politician. He entered politics in 1953 and was Minister of Defence and then Finance in Willy Brandt's government. He replaced Brandt as Chancellor in 1974.

Smith, Ian Douglas (1919-). White Rhodesian leader. In 1964, he became prime minister, pledged to defend white supremacy against black majority rule. He declared independence from Britain in 1965 and successfully defied economic sanctions from the United Nations. But growing guerilla activity

▲ **Andrew Young** talks to reporters.

forced him to seek agreement with moderate black leaders in 1978.

Solzhenitsyn, Alexander (1918-). Russian writer and dissident. His books *A Day in the Life of Ivan Denisovitch* and *The Gulag Archipelago* exposed the tyranny of the Soviet labour camp system. He won the Nobel Prize for Literature in 1970, and was expelled from Russia in 1974.

Thatcher, Mrs Margaret (1925-). Conservative politician in Britain. She became leader of her party on Edward Heath's resignation in 1975, and advocated reducing state power and restoring individual initiative. She won the 1979 election to become Britain's first woman prime minister.

Vorster, Balthazar Johannes (1915-). South African prime minister. He was a member of the pro-Nazi Afrikaner movement during World War Two. Appointed prime minister in 1966, he continued to support rigid apartheid. In 1978, his government was hit by financial scandal and he retired.

Wilson, Harold (1916-). British Labour Party politician. He led the party from 1963-74, skilfully holding together its right and left wings. He was prime minister from 1964-70. Re-elected in 1974, he resigned unexpectedly two years later. He was knighted in 1976.

Woodward, Bob (1943-) and **Bernstein**, Carl (1944-). American journalists, known together as "Woodstein". Their investigation of the Watergate affair for the *Washington Post* eventually led to Nixon's resignation. They also wrote two best selling books, *All the President's Men* and *The Final Days*, about Watergate.

Young, Andrew Jackson (1932-). US diplomat. An early supporter of Martin Luther King's civil rights movement, he became a congressman for Atlanta. Carter appointed him Ambassador to the United Nations, where his outspoken support for black nationalist movements made him a controversial figure. Young was forced to resign in 1979.

The Main Events

The decade was dominated by the oil crisis. The sixties were said to be swinging years. The seventies were more sober.

▲ Hotpants, 1971

▲ Israeli artillery, Sinai, 1973

▲ Watergate tapes are handed over, 1974

1970
January: Biafran war in Nigeria ends.
March: Prince Sihanouk is overthrown in Cambodia.
April: the United States and South Vietnam invade Cambodia to counter North Vietnamese build-up there. Apollo 13 mission is checked in midflight because of explosion; astronauts return safely. China launches her first satellite.
June: Labour loses British general election; Conservative Edward Heath becomes prime minister. Brazil wins World Cup.
September: war in Jordan between King Hussein and Palestinians; guerillas hi-jack four planes and blow up three. President Nasser dies in Egypt, is succeeded by Anwar Sadat.
October: Marxist Salvador Allende is elected president in Chile.
November: United States resumes bombing North Vietnam. General de Gaulle dies. Cyclone and floods devastate East Pakistan.
General
Film: *Butch Cassidy and the Sundance Kid.*

1971
January: Idi Amin's military coup in Uganda. China is admitted to the United Nations.
February: decimalization is introduced in Britain. Mrs Gandhi wins general election in India. East Pakistan breaks away from West.
April: Russia launches Salyut space laboratory.
June: three Russian cosmonauts link up with Salyut but are found dead on return to earth.
August: heaviest rioting for 50 years in Northern Ireland as government announces internment without trial for suspected terrorists.
September: Tupamaros guerillas in Uruguay free British ambassador after eight months' captivity. Former Russian leader, Nikita Khrushchev dies.
October: British House of Commons votes in favour of joining the Common Market.
December: war between India and Pakistan; Pakistan surrenders unconditionally.
General
Film: Stanley Kubrick's *Clockwork Orange.*
Musical: *Jesus Christ Superstar.*

1972
January: unemployment in Britain reaches one million. British troops kill 13 civilians in Bloody Sunday disturbances in Northern Ireland.
February: President Nixon visits China.
March: Britain imposes direct rule from Westminster on Northern Ireland.
May: Strategic Arms Limitation Treaty (SALT 1) is signed by the United States and Russia.
August: Amin expels 40,000 Ugandan Asians. They flee to Britain.
September: 17 people die in Palestinian terrorist attack at the Munich Olympics. Norway votes to stay out of the Common Market.
November: President Nixon is re-elected in the United States.
December: Gough Whitlam becomes the first Labour prime minister in Australia.
General
Film: Coppola's *The Godfather.*
Exhibition: 1.6 million people visit the Tutankhamun Exhibition at the British Museum.

1973
January: Vietnam ceasefire agreement provides for talks between North and South. Britain, Denmark and Ireland join the Common Market.
March: a referendum in Northern Ireland shows an overwhelming majority for maintaining links with Britain. The last US troops leave Vietnam.
May: American astronauts dock with Skylab.
June: drought and famine in Ethiopia.
August: Watergate cover-up begins to be exposed.
September: Henry Kissinger becomes US Secretary of State. Allende overthrown in Chile.
October: Middle East War breaks out. Juan Peron becomes president in Argentina. American vice-president, Spiro Agnew, resigns after income tax scandal. Oil prices are doubled.
December: IRA bomb attacks on British cities. Gerald Ford becomes American vice-president. Britain is reduced to a three-day working week because of the energy crisis and miners' strike.
General
Novel: Richard Adams, *Watership Down.*

1974
February: the Conservatives lose Britain's general election; Harold Wilson becomes prime minister for the third time. Alexander Solzhenitsyn is expelled from Russia.
April: Portugal's dictatorship is overthrown in a left-wing army coup.
May: Giscard d'Estaing becomes French president. Helmut Schmidt becomes West German chancellor.
June: Golda Meir resigns as prime minister in Israel; Yitzhal Rabin succeeds her.
July: Turkey invades Cyprus. The Greek junta collapses; Constantine Karamanlis takes over.
August: Nixon resigns as President of the United States; Gerald Ford replaces him.
September: Emperor Haile Selassie is deposed by an army coup in Ethiopia.
October: Labour wins Britain's general election. Muhammad Ali regains world heavyweight title.
General
Film: Friedkin's *The Exorcist.*
Space: Mariner 10 transmits pictures of Mercury.

1975
January: Sheikh Mujibur Rahman is assassinated in Bangladesh.
March: King Faisal of Saudi Arabia is assassinated by his nephew.
April: the Vietnam War ends in victory for the North. The Khmer Rouge take over in Cambodia.
June: Mrs Gandhi declares a State of Emergency in India. The Suez Canal is re-opened to international shipping. The former Portuguese colonies of Mozambique and Angola become independent. Britain votes to stay in the EEC.
July: the Apollo-Soyuz link-up takes place.
October: fighting breaks out between Christians and Muslims in Lebanon. Russia's Venus 10 soft-lands on Venus. The Nobel Peace Prize is awarded to the Russian dissident, Andrei Sakharov.
November: General Franco dies in Spain; monarchy is restored under Prince Juan Carlos.
General
Film: Spielberg's *Jaws.*
Energy: Britain receives her first North Sea oil.

1976

January: Chinese prime minister Chou En-lai dies; Hua Kuo-feng succeeds. Concorde flights begin.
March: Isabel Peron is overthrown in Argentina.
April: James Callaghan succeeds Harold Wilson as British prime minister.
June: blacks riot at Soweto in South Africa.
July: United States celebrate bi-centenary. Israeli commandos raid Entebbe airport.
September: Chairman Mao dies in China; Hua Kuo-feng succeeds.
October: British Rail introduces High Speed Train. Gang of Four is arrested in China.
November: Jimmy Carter is elected US president.
General
Film: Pakula's *All the President's Men*.
Popular craze for Kung Fu films.
Novel: Alex Haley, *Roots*.
History: last volume of Solzhenitsyn's *The Gulag Archipelago*.
Space: Viking 1 transmits pictures from Mars.

1977

February: Britain celebrates Silver Jubilee.
March: Mrs Gandhi is defeated in India.
April: German Baader-Meinhof terrorists are sentenced to life imprisonment.
May: Begin becomes Israeli prime minister.
June: democratic elections take place in Spain.
July: an army coup topples President Bhutto in Pakistan. Eritrea rebels against Ethiopia.
August: Khmer Rouge commit atrocities in Cambodia.
September: black South African leader Steve Biko dies in police detention. First cheap Skytrain flights take place.
November: President Sadat goes on peace mission to Israel. Russia celebrates the 60th anniversary of the Bolshevik Revolution.
December: Vietnam and Cambodia clash.
General
Novel: John Fowles's *Daniel Martin*.
Film: Lucas's *Star Wars*; Allen's *Annie Hall*.
Space: space shuttle tests begin. Voyager craft is launched to Saturn and Jupiter.

1978

February: Charter 77 dissident group accuses Czech government of violating human rights.
March: *Amoco Cadiz* oil tanker disaster occurs.
April: Vietnam expels its Chinese population.
May: 700 blacks and 136 whites are slaughtered by invading rebels in Zaire. Former Italian prime minister Aldo Moro is murdered by Red Brigades.
June: Argentina wins World Cup.
July: first test tube baby is born in Britain.
September: Camp David conference results in *Framework for Peace* in the Middle East. Muhammad Ali wins the world heavyweight boxing title for the third time.
October: Polish pope, John Paul II, is elected.
November: 900 followers of Jim Jones commit mass suicide in Guyana. Peking wall posters attack Mao.
December: unrest grows in Iran.
General
Film: Badham's *Saturday Night Fever*.
Musical: Rice and Webber's *Evita*.
Play: Tom Stoppard's *Night and Day*.

1979

January: Vietnamese invaders overthrow Khmer Rouge in Cambodia. Tanzania invades Uganda.
February: war breaks out between China and Vietnam. The Shah flees Iran; Ayatollah Khomeini returns from exile to form republic.
April: Bhutto is executed in Pakistan. A radiation leak occurs at Three Mile Island.
May: SALT 2 is signed by the United States and Russia. Bishop Muzorewa becomes Rhodesia's first black premier, but the guerilla war goes on.
June: Idi Amin flees Uganda. Pope John Paul II visits Poland. The first direct elections to the European Parliament take place.
August: Skylab falls to earth in Australia.
September: Rhodesian peace talks begin in London. Bokassa is ousted from the Central African Empire.
October: starvation in Cambodia.
November: Iranian students hold US embassy officials hostage.
December: Rhodesian peace talks end. Russian troops occupy Afghanistan.

▲ **FNLA guerillas in training, Angola 1977**

▲ **Anti-Shah riots, Iran, 1978**

▲ **Punks photographed in 1979**

The World Economy

Inflation and recession were twin problems of the period. They hit all countries, rich or poor. Thirty years of steady prices and steady growth ended.

Annual increases in inflation since 1969 (figures in percentages)

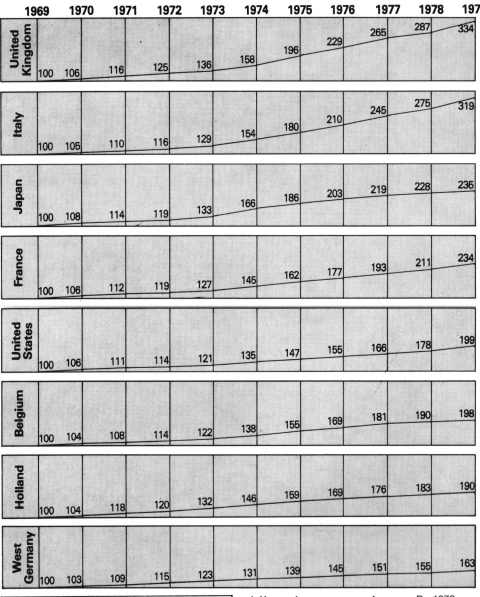

	1969	1970	1971	1972	1973	1974	1975	1976	1977	1978	1979
United Kingdom	100	106	116	125	136	158	196	229	265	287	334
Italy	100	105	110	116	129	154	180	210	245	275	319
Japan	100	108	114	119	133	166	186	203	219	228	235
France	100	106	112	119	127	145	162	177	193	211	234
United States	100	106	111	114	121	135	147	155	166	178	199
Belgium	100	104	108	114	122	138	155	169	181	190	198
Holland	100	104	118	120	132	146	159	169	176	183	190
West Germany	100	103	109	115	123	131	139	145	151	155	163

Average annual inflation, 1969–79

United Kingdom 13%
Italy 12.4%
Japan 9%
France 8.9%
United States 7.2%
Belgium 7.1%
Holland 7%
West Germany 5%

▲ **How prices rose, year by year.** By 1979, British inflation had risen to 334% of her 1969 figure. That is, goods costing £1.00 in 1969 now cost, on average, £3.34.

Notice that the graphs tend to rise more steeply after the Arab oil embargo of 1973.

◄ **These figures** show the average yearly price rises. But rates of inflation varied. Before 1973, all of these countries had rates of less than 10%. In the following years prices soared. Japanese inflation rose to 24% in 1974, as did Britain's in 1975.

Inflation is a situation in which prices rise continuously and money loses its value. Recession is a slowdown in trade and in the production of goods.

The main reason for these two problems was the reduced supply, and soaring price, of oil. The crisis began in 1973, in the wake of the Middle East War.

Oil provided fuel for transport and industry. Several products such as plastics were themselves by-products of oil. Since production, transport and materials cost more, so did a huge variety of goods.

Oil prices hit east and west alike. Russia's oil production was falling, and her East European allies joined in the scramble for scarce supplies.

Poor nations with little industry suffered too. Since they bought goods from the industrialized nations, high prices were passed on to them.

Enormous amounts of money poured in to the Arab countries and wealthy Arabs were seen more and more spending freely in western cities.

But the Arab nations could not spend *all* their new wealth on foreign goods. So there was, overall, less money in the industrialized nations to stimulate economic activity. This in turn led to lower production and unemployment.

These problems, however, did not affect everyone equally. West Germany's efficient economy survived the oil crisis with relatively low inflation. The United States suffered because of her high oil consumption. She ceased to be the world's economic strong man.

Britain was badly hit because she relied on old, declining industries like shipbuilding and textiles. Her car industry was affected by labour unrest. Although British industry was in decline, her workers wanted to keep pace with rising prices by demanding higher wages; this in turn led to further inflation.

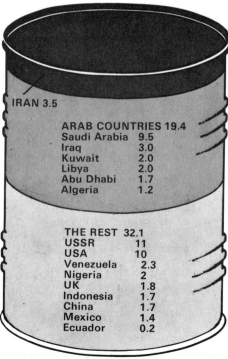

▲ **Dutch cartoon of 1973** showing an Arab holding world leaders to ransom (Brandt of West Germany, Pompidou of France, Nixon of the United States and Heath of Britain).

The industrialized nations resented the oil price rises. But the Arabs were only putting a realistic value on their main commodity. Western nations could no longer rely on buying cut-price fuel and raw materials.

Oil production (millions of barrels per day)

IRAN 3.5

ARAB COUNTRIES 19.4	
Saudi Arabia	9.5
Iraq	3.0
Kuwait	2.0
Libya	2.0
Abu Dhabi	1.7
Algeria	1.2

THE REST 32.1	
USSR	11
USA	10
Venezuela	2.3
Nigeria	2
UK	1.8
Indonesia	1.7
China	1.7
Mexico	1.4
Ecuador	0.2

▲ **Unemployed car workers** queue overnight for jobs, Detroit, 1976. Unemployment figures soared in the United States.

▶ **World oil production** (figures for November 1979). More than 40% of it comes from Iran and the Arab countries.

Index

Further Reading

Available in the United States:
COOK, CHRIS and STEVENSON, JOHN, *The Atlas of Modern Warfare*,
    Putnam, 1978
COOKE, ALISTAIR, *The Americans*, Knopf, 1979
GREER, GERMAINE, *The Female Eunuch*, McGraw-Hill, 1971
HACKETT, GENERAL SIR JOHN and others, *The Third World War—
    a Future History*, Macmillan, 1979
HOCKNEY, DAVID, *David Hockney*, Stangos, Nikos, ed. Abrams, 1977
BERNSTEIN, CARL and WOODWARD, BOB, *All the President's Men*,
    Simon and Schuster, 1974; *The Final Days*, Simon and Schuster, 1976
INSIGHT TEAM OF THE LONDON SUNDAY TIMES, *The Yom Kippur War*,
    Doubleday, 1974
JONES-GRIFFITH, PHILIP, *Vietnam Inc.*, Macmillan, 1971
KISSINGER, HENRY, *The White House Years*, Little, Brown, 1979
LACEY, ROBERT, *Majesty*, Harcourt, Brace, Jovanovich, 1977
LAQUER, WALTER, *Terrorism*, Little, Brown, 1977; *The Guerilla Reader:
    A Historical Anthology*, Temple University Press, 1977
MILLETT, KATE, *Sexual Politics*, Ballantine, 1978
NAIPAUL, V. S., *India: A Wounded Civilization*, Knopf, 1977
NIXON, RICHARD, *Memoirs*, Grosset and Dunlap, 1978
PALMER, ALAN, *The Penguin Dictionary of Twentieth Century History:
    1900–1978*, Penguin Books, 1979
RABAN, JONATHAN, *Arabia Through the Looking Glass*, Simon and
    Schuster, 1979
SHAWCROSS, WILLIAM, *Sideshow: Kissinger, Nixon and the Destruction
    of Cambodia*, Simon and Schuster, 1971
SOLZHENITSYN, ALEXANDER, *One Day in the Life of Ivan Denisovitch*,
    Dutton, 1971; *The Gulag Archipelago* (vols 1–3), Harper-Row, 1979;
    Warning to the West, Farrar, Straus and Giroux, 1976
WHITE, THEODORE, *The Making of the President*, 1972, Atheneum, 1973
WOLFE, TOM, *The Right Stuff*, Farrar, Straus and Giroux, 1979

Available in Britain:
COOK, CHRIS and STEVENSON, JOHN, *The Atlas of Modern Warfare*,
    Weidenfeld and Nicolson, 1978
COOKE, ALISTAIR, *The Americans*, Bodley Head, 1979
EVANS, CHRISTOPHER, *The Mighty Micro*, Gollancz, 1979.
GREER, GERMAINE, *The Female Eunuch*, MacGibbon and Kee, 1970.
GRIFFITHS, PHILIP, *Vietnam Inc.*, Collier-Macmillan, 1972.
HACKETT, GENERAL SIR JOHN and others, *The Third World War—a
    future history*, Sidgwick and Jackson, 1978.
HOCKNEY, DAVID, *Hockney by Hockney*, Thames and Hudson, 1976.
INSIGHT TEAM, SUNDAY TIMES, *The Yom Kippur War*, Deutsch, 1975.
KISSINGER, HENRY, *The White House Years*, Weidenfeld and Nicolson,
    1979.
LACEY, ROBERT, *Majesty*, Hutchinson, 1977.
LAQUEUR, WALTER, *Terrorism*, Weidenfeld and Nicolson, 1977;
    Guerilla, Weidenfeld and Nicolson, 1977.
MEREDITH, MARTIN, *The Past is Another Country*, Deutsch, 1979.
MILLETT, KATE, *Sexual Politics*, Hart Davis, 1971.
NAIPAUL, V. S., *India—a Wounded Civilization*, Deutsch, 1977.
NIXON, RICHARD, *Memoirs*, Sidgwick and Jackson, 1978.
PALMER, ALAN, *The Penguin Dictionary of 20th Century History*,
    1900-1978, Penguin Books, 1979.
RABAN, JONATHAN, *Arabia Through the Looking Glass*, Collins, 1979.
SHAWCROSS, WILLIAM, *Sideshow: Kissinger, Nixon and the Destruction
    of Cambodia*, Deutsch, 1979.
SOLZHENITSYN, ALEXANDER, *One Day in the Life of Ivan Denisovitch*,
    Bodley Head, 1971; *The Gulag Archipelago* (vols 1-3), Collins Harvill,
    1974, 1975, 1978; *Warning to the Western World*, Bodley Head, 1976.
WHITE, THEODORE, *The Making of the President*, 1972, Cape, 1973.
WOLFE, TOM, *The Right Stuff*, Cape, 1979.
WOODWARD, ROBERT and BERNSTEIN, CARL, *All the President's Men*,
    Secker and Warburg, 1974; *The Final Days*, Secker and Warburg, 1976

Acknowledgements

We wish to thank the following individuals
and organizations for their assistance and
for making available material in their
collections.

Key to picture positions:
(T) top; (C) centre; (B) bottom; (R) right;
(L) left, and combinations, for example, (TC)
top centre.

Brian Alford *17(BR)*
Associated Press *8(B), 12, 22(T), 23(T), (BR),
    36, 37(BR)*
Chris Barker *47(B)*
R. Bedi/Camera Press *21(TL)*
Colin Beer/Daily Telegraph Colour Library *16(B)*
F. Behrendt *61(BR)*
Adrian Boot/London Features International
    31(T)
Giancarlo Botti/Camera Press *14(L), 58(T)*
British Aerospace *3*
British Posters *48*
Camera Press, *6, 7(BR), 19(B), 20(BL), 21(BL),
    27(BL), 38(BR), 39(TR), 42(TL), (BL),
    45(TR), 49(TL), (TR), (B), 52(T), (B), 54(B),
    57(L), (C), 58(C)*
Tim Canadine *19(TL), (CL)*
Daily Telegraph Colour Library *38(TL), (B),
    39(TL)*
R. E. Dear/Daily Telegraph Colour Library
    25(BR)
European Communities Commission *32(T)*
Mick Fallowfield/Private Eye *16(T)*
Sally Fear/Camera Press *15(BR)*
Ferranti/Rowlinsen/Broughten *44(T)*
Fiat *44(B)*
Leonard Freed/Magnum *34*
Friends of the Earth (photo Chris Barker)

13(TR), (B)
Martyn Goddard/Daily Telegraph Colour Library
    42-3
Ray Green/Camera Press *33(CR)*
Hemdale, *29(TL)*
Henson Associates Inc., 1979, *28(T)*
John Hillelson Agency *10(B), 41(T), 55(T)*
Anthony Howarth/Daily Telegraph Colour
    Library *45(TL)*
Reto Hugin/Camera Press *21(BR)*
Colin Jones/Camera Press *59(B)*
Keystone Press *51(T), 53(T)*
Peter Knapp/Daily Telegraph Colour Library
    15(TL)
Alain Le Garsmeur/Camera Press *25(T)*
London Features International Ltd *30(TR),
    31(CR)*
Leo Mason/Daily Telegraph Colour Library *2*
NASA/Associated Press *46(T)*
Paramount Pictures Corporation *30-31*
Chris Perkins/Viva *20(BR)*
Popperfoto *4(T), 7(C), 9(B), 13(TL), 22(B),
    53(TR), 54(T), 55(BL), (BC), (BR),
    56(L), 57(R), 58(B), 61(BL)*
Punch *7(BL), 13(CL), 15(TR), 24(B), 49(C)*
Michael Putland/London Features International
    Ltd *30(B)*
Rex Features *4(B), 5(T), 7(T), 9(T), 10(T), 10-11,
    11(TL), (TR), 17(BL), 19(TR), 24(TL), 24-5,
    27(CR), 29(CL), 33(B), 37(BL), 39(B), 40-41,
    43(T), 44-5, 50(B), 50-51, 56(R), 59(T), (C)*
L.L.T. Rhodes/Daily Telegraph Colour Library
    26, 27(BR)
John Richardson/Skillet Sailing School *37(TL)*
John Rigby/Daily Telegraph Colour Library
    27(TL)
Anthea Sieveking/Vision International *14(R)*
Shaun Skelly *43(C)*
Stiff Records/Polydor/Chrysalis/CBS/Liberty

United (photo Chris Barker) *31(B)*
Homer Sykes *15(BL)*
Tate Gallery *43(B)*
Macdonald/Maggie Murray *27(TR)*
John Urry/Daily Telegraph Colour Library *18*
Nick Wheeler/Daily Telegraph Colour Library *1*
Andrew Wiard/Report *33(CL)*
Eric Wilkins/Daily Telegraph Colour Library *33(T)*
John Zylinski *35*
Lucas Film UK Ltd *29(CR)*

Artists
Peter Acty *p.4-5, 8(T), 20(T), 27(BL), 32(BL),
    37(TR), 50(TL), 53(BR), 60, 61*
Tony Payne *p.17(T), 46, 47*

Editor
Tim Healey

Production
Rosemary Bishop

Picture research
Georgina Barker

Front cover: the microchip, perhaps the most
significant technological innovation of the
seventies (Ferranti-Broughten-Rowlinsen).

Back cover: A punk rocker (Homer Sykes).

If we have unwittingly infringed copyright in any
picture or photograph reproduced in this
publication, we tender our sincerest apologies
and will be glad of the opportunity, upon being
satisfied as to the owner's title, to pay an
appropriate fee as if we had been able to obtain
prior permission.